Contents

Front cover: Micklegate Bar, York

Introduction

This bibliography is intended primarily for genealogists. It is, however, hoped that it will also prove useful to historians, librarians, archivists, research students, and anyone else interested in the history of Yorkshire. It is intended to be used in conjunction with my *English genealogy: a bibliography,* and the other volumes in the *British genealogical library guides* series. A full list of these volumes currently in print appears on the back cover.

This volume lists published parish registers, monumental inscriptions, and probate records relating to the historic county of Yorkshire. Volume 1 is devoted to general information on the county's history, bibliography, archives, journals, *etc.,* other categories of source material for the county are listed in vols. 3-5; pedigrees, family histories, *etc.,* are listed in vol.6. The whole work is exclusively concerned with published works, and thousands of books and journal articles are listed. Numerous microfiche publications are also listed. However, the innumerable notes and queries to be found in family history society journals *etc.,* are excluded, except where their content is of importance. Where I have included such notes, replies to them are cited in the form 'see also', with no reference to the names of respondents. I have also excluded extracts from newspapers, and works which have not been published. It should be noted that many libraries, such as the Society of Genealogists, hold unpublished transcripts of parish registers, monumental inscriptions, *etc.,* not listed here. Where possible, citations are accompanied by notes indicating the period covered, the locality/ies in which the families concerned dwelt, and other pertinent information. I have physically examined almost every item listed here; those which have not been seen are annotated 'not seen', as I have not been able to check the correct title or the contents.

Be warned: just because information has been published, it does not necessarily follow that it is accurate. I have not made any judgement on the accuracy of most works listed: that is up to you.

Anyone who tries to compile a totally comprehensive bibliography of Yorkshire is likely to fall short of his aim. The task is almost impossible, especially if the endeavour is made by one person. That does not, however, mean that the attempt should not be made. Usefulness, rather than comprehensiveness, has been my prime aim — and this book would not be useful to anyone if its publication were to be prevented by a vain attempt to ensure total comprehensiveness. I am well aware that there are likely to be omissions, especially in view of the fact that, given constraints of time and money, it has not been possible for me to visit all of the large number of libraries with substantial collections on Yorkshire's history. Each of them may well possess works not held anywhere else. The identification of such works is not, however, a major aim of this bibliography. Rather, my purpose has been to enable you to identify works which are mostly readily available. Some titles you may be able to purchase; all can be found in libraries throughout the English-speaking world. You can check the holdings of many libraries via their catalogues on the internet; alternatively, if your local library does not hold a particular book, the librarian should be able to tell you where to find it — and, as a last resort, may be able to borrow it for you via the inter-library loan network, irrespective of whether you live in London or San Francisco. The libraries of family history societies are also worth checking — even if they are far distant from Yorkshire: for example, the Genealogical Society of Victoria, in Melbourne, has a good collection of books on English genealogy. Some family history societies offer a postal borrowing service; others may be willing to check a particular book for you. It is also worth joining one of the genealogical newsgroups or mailing lists on the internet; other members may hold the books you need, and be willing to check them for you.

If you are an assiduous researcher, you may well come across items I have missed. If you do, please let me know, so that they can be included in the next edition.

The work of compiling this bibliography has depended heavily on the resources of the libraries I have used. These included the local studies collections in the public libraries of Bradford, Doncaster, Hull, Leeds, Sheffield, and York, the Brotherton Library at the University of Leeds, the British Library, the Society of Genealogists, Guildhall Library, the University and the Central Library in Bristol, the University of Exeter library and the Exeter Public Library in Exeter. I have also used the resources of a number of family history societies, and am particularly grateful to the societies for Devon, Cornwall, Somerset & Dorset, Sheffield and Ripon/Harrogate. All these institutions deserve my thanks, as does John Perkins, who read and commented on an early draft of the book. Paul

Raymond, Mary Raymond, and Cynthia Hanson typed the manuscript, and Bob Boyd saw the book through the press. I am grateful too to the officers of the Federation of Family History Societies, whose support is vital for the continuation of this series. My thanks also to my wife Marjorie.

Stuart A. Raymond

Abbreviations

B.A.	*Bradford antiquary*
B.I.B.	*Borthwick Institute bulletin.*
B.S.H.S.	*Bulletin of the Saddleworth Historical Society.*
B.T.	*Banyan tree: journal of the East Yorkshire Family History Society.*
B.T.C.	Borthwick texts and calendars: records of the Northern Provinces.
Bk.I.H.R	*Borthwick Institute of Historical Records*
C.R.S.	*Catholic Record Society.*
C.T.L.H.S.B.	*Cleveland and Teeside Local History Society bulletin.*
C.Y.D.F.H.S.J.	*City of York & District Family History Society Journal.*
Cameo	*Cameo: Morley & District Family History Group newsletter.*
Don. Anc.	*Doncaster ancestor.*
E.Y.F.H.S.	East Yorkshire Family History Society
E.Y.F.H.S., M.I.	East Yorkshire Family History Society monumental inscriptions.
E.Y.L.H.S.	East Yorkshire Local History Society series
F.H.S.	Family History Society
F.S.	*Flowing stream: journal of Sheffield & District Family History Society*
H. & D.F.H.S.	Huddersfield & District Family History Society
H. & D.F.H.S.J.	*Huddersfield & District Family History Society journal*
J.Cl.F.H.S.	*Journal of the Cleveland Family History Society*
K.D.F.H.S.J.	*Keighley & District Family History Society journal*
M.G.H.	*Miscellanea genealogica et heraldica*
N. & Q.	*Notes and queries: a quarterly magazine ... South Yorkshire*
N.H.	*Northern history*
O.W.R.	*Old West Riding*
P.R.H.A.S.	*Papers, reports, etc., read before the Halifax Antiquarian Society.*
R.D.F.H.S.N.	*Rotherham & District Family History Society newsletter*

R.H.	*Ripon Historian*
T.E.R.A.S.	*Transactions of the East Riding Archaeological Society*
T.Hal.A.S.	*Transactions of the Halifax Archaeological Society*
T.Hunter A.S.	*Transactions of the Hunter Archaeological Society.*
T.R.S.	*Teesdale Record Society [proceedings].*
T.S.	Thoresby Society
Wh.N.	*Wharfedale newsletter: the journal of the Wharfedale Family History Group.*
Y.A.J.	*Yorkshire archaeological journal*
Y.A.S.	Yorkshire Archaeological Society
Y.A.S., F.H.P.S.S.	Yorkshire Archaeological Society. Family History and Population Studies Section
Y.A.S., F.H.P.S.S.N.	*Yorkshire Archaeological Society. Family History and Population Studies Section Newsletter.*
Y.A.S., P.R.S.	Yorkshire Archaeological Society. Parish Register Section
Y.A.S., R.S.	Yorkshire Archaeological Society. Record Series
Y.C.M.	*Yorkshire county magazine*
Y.F.H.	*Yorkshire family historian*
Y.F.H.S.N.	*York Family History Society Newsletter*
Y.G.	*Yorkshire genealogist*
Y.N.Q. I.	*Yorkshire notes & queries* [1888-90]
Y.N.Q. II.	*Yorkshire notes & queries* [1905-9]
Y.P.R.S.	Yorkshire Parish Register Society

Bibliographic Presentation

Authors names are in SMALL CAPITALS. Book and journal titles are in *italics*. Articles appearing in journals, and material such as parish register transcripts, forming only part of books are in inverted commas and textface type. Volume numbers are in **bold** and the individual number of the journal may be shown in parentheses. These are normally followed by the place of publication (except where this is London, which is omitted), the name of the publisher and the date of publication. In the case of articles, further figures indicate page numbers.

Libraries and Record Offices

Many libraries have substantial collections of books and journals on Yorkshire history, and the addresses given below are only amongst the most important. I have not included the addresses of most family history societies, most of which have libraries available to members, which ought to be used by everyone tracing their ancestors in the area covered. These addresses change frequently, and any listing would be out of date by the time it was printed. Current addresses are regularly published in *Family history news & digest*.

I have also not included the addresses of most Yorkshire record repositories. These hold the archives you may need to consult, but generally speaking do not have large collections of printed books.

It is also worth pointing out that many public and university libraries throughout the English-speaking world hold much Yorkshire material; in particular, many university libraries subscribe to major series such as the *Yorkshire archaeological journal* and the Yorkshire Archaeological Society's *Record series* — which may also be available in the libraries of other county historical societies, many of which exchange journals with each other.

Major collections of Yorkshire material are to be found in at least two London institutions:

British Library
96, Euston Road,
London,
NW1 2DB

Society of Genealogists,
14, Charterhouse Buildings,
Goswell Road,
London,
EC1M 7BA

The two Yorkshire institutions with a county-wide remit are:

Borthwick Institute,
University of York,
St.Anthony's Hall
Peasholme Green,
York,
YO1 2PW

Yorkshire Archaeological Society
Claremont,
23, Clarendon Road,
Leeds,
LS2 9NZ

A number of university libraries in the county have important Yorkshire collections:

Brynmor Jones Library,
University of Hull,
Hull, HU6 7RX
(Houses the East Yorkshire Bibliography)

Brotherton Library
University of Leeds
Leeds, LS2 9JT

The major local collections in public libraries are:

Bradford
Bradford Central Library
Princes Way,
Bradford,
BD1 1NN

Hull
Local Studies Library,
Hull Central Library
Albion Street,
Hull, HU1 3TF

Leeds
Local History Collection,
Central Library,
Calverley Street,
Leeds, LS1 3AB

Middlesbrough
Local Collection,
Middlesbrough Reference Library,
Victoria Square,
Middlesbrough,
Cleveland,
TS1 2AY

Sheffield
Local Studies Library,
Sheffield City Libraries,
Surrey Street,
Sheffield, S1 1XZ

York
York City Library,
Reference Library,
Local Studies Collection,
Museum Street,
York, YO1 2DS

1. PARISH REGISTERS AND OTHER RECORDS OF BIRTHS, MARRIAGES AND DEATHS.

Parish registers are usually the first port of call for genealogists tracing ancestors prior to 1837. A variety of guides to them have been published; the authoritative listing (which also includes bishops transcripts, nonconformist registers, etc) is:

WILCOX, ANTHONY. *National index of parish registers, volume II, part 2. Yorkshire: North and East Ridings and York.* Society of Genealogists, 1998.

WILCOX, ANTHONY. *National index of parish registers ... Volume II, part 3. Yorkshire, West Riding.* Society of Genealogists, 1998.

See also the equally up to date:

WITHERS, COLIN BLANSHARD. *Yorkshire parish registers, volume I. Church of England.* Bainton: Yorkshire Wolds Publications, 1998.

An older listing, which also includes monumental inscriptions, is:

BELT, ANN. *Whereabouts of Yorkshire parish records.* 2 vols. Occasional paper 2. Leeds: Y.A.S., F.H.P.S.S., 1986. Despite the title, this lists parish and nonconformist registers and indexes, monumental inscriptions, and a handful of other items only.

For a brief discussion of Yorkshire parish registers, with many extracts, see:

WHITING, C.E. 'Parish registers, with special reference to those of Yorkshire,' *Y.A.J.* **37**, 1951, 131-44.

See also:

SMITH, LESLIE. *Parish gleanings: curiosities from local parish registers.* Occasional series 1. Doncaster: Doncaster & District F.H.S., 1996. A 'pot pourri' of curiosities.

Chronicon mirabile, or, extracts from parish registers, principally in the North of England. J.B.Nicholls and Son, 1841. Brief extracts from parish registers, principally from Co. Durham and Northumberland, with a few from Yorkshire and other counties, 16-17th c.

WOODWARD, DONALD. 'The impact of the Commonwealth act on Yorkshire parish registers', *Local population studies* **14**, 1975, 15-31. Study of registers in the 1650's.

Bishops' Transcripts

Bishops' transcripts provide a useful supplement to parish registers, enabling checks of their accuracy to be made, and providing back-up where original registers are missing. They are listed by Wilcox (see above). Those for the Diocese of York are now in the Borthwick Institute of Historical Research, and are listed in:

GURNEY, NORAH K.M. *A handlist of parish register transcripts in the Borthwick Institute of Historical Research.* B.T.C. 3. York: Bk.I.H.R., 1976.

This supersedes:

HUDSON, A.V., & WALKER, J.W. 'Index to the parish register transcripts preserved in the Diocesan Registry, York,' in *Miscellanea* 2. Y.A.S., R.S. 74. 1929.

See also:

G., A. 'Archbishops' transcripts of parish registers at York,' *Northern Genealogist* **5**, 1902, 76-7. Brief note.

RUSBY, JAMES. 'Transcript of parish registers (York Diocesan registry),' *Y.C.M.* **1**, 1891, 14-17. Brief note on bishops' transcripts, with 17th c. extracts from Armthorpe, Felkirk, Kirk Bramwith, Kirk Sandall, Kirk Sweaton, Owston, Warmfield, *etc.*

Nonconformist Registers

Registers of the nonconformist denominations are listed by Wilcox (see above). Reference may also be made to:

HIPWELL, DANIEL. 'Lists of non-parochial registers and records in the custody of the Register General ...,' *Y.C.M.* **2** 1892, 11-22, 81-8 & 155-63; **3**, 1893, 24-9.

DALE, BRYAN. 'Non-parochial registers in Yorkshire', *Transactions of the Congregational History Society* **1**, 1901-4, 5-25. General discussion.

DALE, BRYAN. 'Non-parochial registers in Yorkshire,' *B.A.* N.S. **1**, 1900, 447-69. General discussion of nonconformist registers.

Roman Catholic registers are listed in the invaluable:

GANDY, MICHAEL. *Catholic missions and registers 1700-1880: volume 5. North West England*. Whetstone: Michael Gandy, 1993.

Strays

'Stray' entries from parish registers, i.e. those entries recording events relating to people from other parishes, are frequently printed in family history society journals. Only the more important collections of strays are listed here.

Yorkshire strays index. Fiche. Federation of Family History Societies, 1989-94.

Yorkshire strays. Occasional paper 1. Leeds: Y.A.S., F.H.P.S.S., 1983. From parish registers, marriage licences, monumental inscriptions, *etc*.

Yorkshire strays 2. Part 2, baptisms and burials. Occasional paper 7. Leeds: Y.A.S., F.H.P.S.S., 1988.

CAWLEY, A.P.D. *East Riding strays and strangers*. [ ]: E.Y.F.H.S., 1981.

Strays. 2nd ed. [ ]: E.Y.F.H.S., 1984.

Strays. 3rd ed [ ]: E.Y.F.H.S., 1989. The 2nd edition includes material from the 1st edition, but the 3rd edition is entirely new.

COOKSON, EDWARD. 'Waifs and strays', *Northern notes and queries* 1, 1906, 153-4, 168-9, 209 & 244. Extracts from Yorkshire parish registers relating to Cumberland, Westmorland, Northumberland and Durham.

J[EWERS], A.J. 'Notes from Wells', *Y.C.M.* 3, 1983, 129- 30. Yorkshire extracts from the parish registers of Wells, Somerset.

MARKENDALE, SHEILA. 'Strays from the parish register of St Bartholemew's church, Colne, Lancs,' *K.D.F.H.S.J.* Spring 1996, 16-18.

SKELTON, SANDY. 'Some Yorkshire strays from the marriage registers of the Episcopal Chapel, Haddington, Scotland', *Y.F.H.* 19(3), 1993, 71-2. 1764-92.

PAUL, JEAN. '1892/3 strays from Sanford, Maine,' *Bod-kin* 18, 1990, 10-11. Births, marriages and deaths of Yorkshiremen and women in the U.S.A.

CARTER, JENNIFER. 'Extracts from Victoria's marriage indexes', *Y.F.H.* 19(4), 1993, 90-91. Australia; lists marriages of Yorkshire migrants.

GOODWILL, JUNE. 'Deaths in Victoria of people born in Yorkshire, 1855', *Y.F.H.* 14(5), 1988, 111-12. Australia; list compiled from death certificates.

Marriage Indexes

A number of marriage indexes are mentioned by Wilcox. *Boyds marriage index* is of major importance, and the Yorkshire portion is now available on fiche:

HINDSLEY, NORMAN. *Boyds marriage index for Yorkshire*. 109 fiche. Society of Genealogists, 1996. For parishes covered, see:

BAXTER, JEANNE. 'Boyds marriage index', *Y.F.H.S.N.* 11, 1985, 13-15.

See also:

JOINER, PAUL R. 'Marriage indexes', *J.Cl.F.H.S.* 4(10), 1991, 16-20. Discussion of Boyds marriage index, with list of parishes covered in Co. Durham and North Yorkshire.

The *International genealogical index* is also of major importance. For guidance in using this index, and a list of parishes covered, consult:

Using the IGI in East Yorkshire. Rev. ed. Cottingham: E.Y.F.H.S., 1989.

A very brief surname index to early 16th c. parish registers is provided by:

'Reference to Yorkshire surnames in 1620', *Genealogical quarterly* 25(3), 1959, 99-104.

Marriage Licences

Marriage licences – or, rather, the bonds and allegations which record them – provide another means of checking parish register entries, and of locating ancestors in the past. Those for York Diocese have been extensively indexed, and the indexes listed below should be checked by everyone tracing Yorkshire ancestors at the relevant periods:

'Pavers marriage licences', *Y.A.J.* 7, 1882, 289-304; 9, 1886, 55-70 & 362-79; 10, 1889, 35-50, 169-204 & 445-60; 11, 1891, 209-45; 12, 1893, 116-22, 143-58 & 269-84; 13, 1895, 371-86; 14, 1896-7, 220-38 & 458-506; 16, 1900-1901, 1-37; 17, 1902-3, 155-91; 20, 1908, 68-97. 1567-1628. Also includes schoolmasters and other licences.

Indexed in:
A consolidated index to Paver's marriage licences (1567 to 1630) printed in the Yorkshire Archaeological journal. Extra series **2**. Leeds: Y.A.S., 1912.
Continued in:
CLAY, JOHN WM. *Paver's marriage licences.* Y.A.S. R.S. **40, 43 & 46**. 1909-12. For 1630-1714.
NEWSOME, E.B. *An index to the Archbishop of York's marriage bonds and allegations 1735-1749.* Borthwick lists and indexes **15**. York: Borthwick Institute, 1996.
NEWSOME, E.B. *An index to the Archbishop of York's marriage bonds & allegations 1750-1774.* Borthwick lists and indexes **13**. York: Borthwick Institute, 1994.
NEWSOME, E.B. *An index to the Archbishop of York's marriage bonds & allegations 1765-1779.* Borthwick lists and indexes **10** [York]: Borthwick Institute, 1993.
NEWSOME, E.B. *An index to the Archbishop of York's marriage bonds & allegations, 1780-1789.* [York]: [Borthwick Institute], 1991.
NEWSOME, E.B. *An index to the Archbishop of York's marriage bonds & allegations, 1790-1799.* York: [Borthwick Institute], 1990.
NEWSOME, E.B., & NEWSOME, W.R. *An index to the Archbishop of York's marriage bonds & allegations, 1800-1809.* York: [Borthwick Institute], 1989.
NEWSOME, E.B. & NEWSOME, W.R. *An index to the Archbishop of York's marriage bonds & allegations, 1810-1819.* York: [Borthwick Institute], 1988.
NEWSOME, E.B., & NEWSOME, W.R. *An index to the Archbishop of York's marriage bonds & allegations, 1820-1829.* York: [Borthwick Institute], 1987.
NEWSOME, E.B., & NEWSOME, W.R. *An index to the Archbishop of York's marriage bonds & allegations, 1830-1839.* York: [Borthwick Institute], 1986.
See also:
'York marriage bonds', *Northern genealogist* **2**, 1896, 27-30, 63-6 & 114-7. 18th c.

For marriage bonds in the peculiar jurisdiction of the Dean and Chapter of York, which covered a large number of parishes throughout the county, see:

NEWSOME, E.B., & NEWSOME, W.R., eds. *An index of marriage bonds and allegations in the peculiar jurisdiction of the Dean and Chapter of York, 1613-1839.* [York]: [Borthwick Institute], 1985.
See also:
WHYTEHEAD, T.B. 'Marriage bonds of the Dean and Chapter of York', *Northern genealogist* **2-5**, 1896-1902, *passim.* 16-19th c.

A list of East Riding allegations and bonds, 1757-62, is printed in:
CAWLEY, ANDREA. 'Marriage bonds and allegations', *B.T.* **15**, 1983, 5-8.

For Yorkshire spouses in Lichfield Diocese, 1722-1825, see:
MILNES, GEOFFREY. 'Dean and Chapter (peculiar marriage bonds), Lichfield', *F.S.* **16**(2), 1995, 49-50.

Birth, Marriage and Death Announcements in Newspapers
Bradford
WILLMOTT, ELVIRA. 'Useful indexes: *Bradford Observer* death notices 1834-1900', *Bod-kin* **33**, 1993, 11. Brief notes on a useful index at Bradford Library.

Cleveland
'Death notices', *J.Cl.F.H.S.* **3**(11), 1988, 48-52. From the *North Eastern Daily Gazette,* 24 July - 14 August 1928.
VINCENT, JOHN. 'North Eastern Daily Gazette August 1928: extracts', *J.Cl.F.H.S.* **4**(2), 1989, 47-9. Of births, marriages and deaths.

Keighley
'[Births from the *Keighley news,* 1863-1886]', *K.D.F.H.S.J.* Winter 1993, 7-8.
'From *Keighley News',* *K.D.F.H.S.J.* Autumn 1993, 13-16. Marriage and death notices, 1876-83.
'From the *Keighley News',* *K.D.F.H.S.J.* Summer 1995, 16-17. Births marriages and deaths, 1880s and 1890s.
Deaths, 1862 to 1870 inclusive, indexed from the Keighley news. Keighley: Keighley and District F.H.S., 1997. A further volume covers 1871 to 1876.

Leeds

LUMB, G.D. 'Extracts from the *Leeds Mercury* 1721-1729', in *Miscellanea* [6]. *T.S.* **12**, 1915, 185-233.

'Extracts from the *Leeds Mercury* 1729-1737', in *Miscellanea* [7]. *T.S.* **24**, 1919, 67-109.

LUMB, G.D. 'Extracts from the *Leeds Mercury*, 1737-1742', in *Miscellanea* [8]. *T.S.* **26**, 1924, 64-101.

'Extracts from the *Leeds Mercury*, 1742-1760', in *Miscellanea* [9.] *T.S.* **28**, 1928, 65-80. And from the *Leeds Intelligencer*.

ROOKE, CHARLES S. 'Extracts from the *Leeds Intelligencer*, in *Miscellanea* [2]. *T.S.* **4**. 1895, 227-44. Includes many notices of births, marriages and deaths, *etc.*, for 1754-8.

LUMB, G.D. 'Extracts from the Leeds Intelligencer 1763-1767', in *Miscellanea* [10.] *T.S.* **33**, 1935, 156-227. Includes death notices, plus much other miscellaneous matter. Also from the *Leeds Mercury*.

LUMB, G. DENISON. *Extracts from the Leeds Intelligencer* and the *Leeds Mercury*, 1769-1776. T.S. **38**. 1938.

LUMB, G.D., PLACE, J.B., & BECKWITH, F., eds. *Extracts from the Leeds Intelligencer and the Leeds Mercury, 1777-1782, with an introductory account of the Leeds Intelligencer* 1754-1866. T.S., **40**. 1955.

LUMB, G.D., ed. *Extracts from the Leeds Intelligencer* 1791-1796. T.S. **44**. 1956.

Scarborough

Scarborough, Yorkshire: birth, marriage and death announcements from the local press, 1839-1867. 16 fiche. Cottingham: E.Y.F.H.S., 1997.

York

HAMBROOK, DAPHNE. 'Extracted from the *York Herald* for Saturday January 3rd, 1863', *C.Y.D.F.H.S.J.* **46**, 1998, 9-10. Birth, marriage and death announcements.

MASTERMAN, HARRY. 'Births, marriages and deaths from the Scarborough press, 1839-1867', *B.T.* **73**, 1998, 23-4. Discussion of an indexing project.

Library and Record Office holdings

Many libraries and record offices hold original parish registers, modern transcripts, and printed editions, *etc.* Wilcox is the authoritative guide to what is where; however, quite a number of lists of individual collections, *etc,* have also been published; these are cited here.

Cleveland

'Cleveland County parish registers', *J.Cl.F.H.S.* 2(8), 1984, 8-10. List with locations; also covers part of Co. Durham.

East Riding Archives

Handlist of non-Anglican church records. Beverley: East Riding Archives and Records Service, 1990.

Handlist of Society of Friends and non-parochial registers on microfilm. Publication 4. Beverley: Humberside Archive Service, [199-?]. The originals are in the Public Record Office, classes RG4 and RG6.

Keighley Library

'More news of acquisitions at Keighley Reference Library', *K.D.F.H.S.J.* Summer 1993, 22-3. List of nonconformist registers deposited.

'Holdings at Keighley Reference Library', *K.D.F.H.S.J.* Winter 1995, 22-3. List of additional parish registers.

Leeds Archives

'Bishops' transcripts', *Cameo* 1992, no. 2, 10-11. List of those held by Leeds Archive Dept.

Middlesbrough Library

'Parish register transcripts in Middlesbrough Central Library', *J.Cl.F.H.S.* 1(4), 1981, 78-9; 1(5), 1981, 121. List.

'Printed parish register transcripts in Middlesborough Reference Library', *J.Cl.F.H.S.* 2(6), 1984, insert. See also 2(7), 1984, 5-7. Covers the whole country, but especially strong for Yorkshire (although full citations are not given).

Rotherham Archives
'Rotherham Metropolitan Borough Council Archives & Local Studies: Anglican parish registers', *Don. Anc.* 4(2), 1989, 57-60. List, also includes nonconformist registers.

Rotherham Library
'Yorkshire County Record Office: duplicate copies in Rotherham Central Library', *R & D.F.H.S.N.* 5, 1985, 1-2. List of burial registers on microfilm.

Sheffield Record Office
SHEFFIELD RECORD OFFICE. *Family history guides, No. 3. Bishop's transcripts.* Sheffield: Sheffield City Libraries, [198-?]
SHEFFIELD ARCHIVES. *Family history guides no 4. Parish registers.* Sheffield: Sheffield City Libraries, [198-?]
SHEFFIELD RECORD OFFICE. *Family history guides no. 5. Copies of parish registers held by other record offices.* Sheffield: Sheffield City Libraries, [198-?]
SHEFFIELD RECORD OFFICE. *Family history guides, No. 6. Non-conformist registers.* Sheffield: Sheffield City Libraries, [198-?]
SHEFFIELD RECORD OFFICE. *Family history guides, No. 8. Registers of burials in churchyards, chapelyards and cemeteries.* Sheffield: Sheffield City Libraries, [198-?]
'Deposited parish records: Sheffield City Libraries Archives Division', *F.S.* 3(4), 1982, 82-3. List of parish registers.

Stockton Library
'Parish register transcripts in Stockton Ref. Library', *J.Cl.F.H.S.* 2(11), 1985, 25-6. All relate to Yorkshire.
JAMES, DAVID. *West Yorkshire Archive Service: guide for family historians: a list of parish, nonconformist, and other related records held by the West Yorkshire Archive Service.* Wakefield: West Yorkshire Joint Services Committee, 1992. Lists registers held by record offices at Bradford, Calderdale, Kirklees, Leeds and Wakefield; also includes valuable introduction describing other related records. Comes in slip-case with a separate map of parish boundaries.

York Library
BUTLER, PETER. 'Parish registers at York Library', *B.T.* 42, 1990, 8-9. List of photocopies.

Yorkshire Archaeological Society
List of parish registers held at Claremont, including printed parish registers and parish register transcripts. 2nd ed. Leeds: Y.A.S., 1996.

Local Registers

Aberford
LUMB, GEORGE DENISON, ed. *The parish register of Aberford, Co. York (1540-1812).* T.S. 36. 1937.

Ackworth
MORTON, DAVE, & MORTON, SANDRA. *St. Cuthbert's parish church, Ackworth, in the West Riding of Yorkshire: marriage index 1813-1837.* Pontefract: Pontefract & District F.H.S., [1998?]
MORTON, SANDRA. *St. Cuthbert's parish church, Ackworth, in the West Riding of Yorkshire: burials 1813-1869.* Pontefract: Pontefract & District F.H.S., 1998.
SAYWELL, J.L 'Yorkshire parish registers', *Y.N.Q.I.* 1, 1888, 107-18. Primarily a transcript of Ackworth register, 1558-86.
SAYWELL, J.L. 'Ackworth registers, 1586-1600', *Y.N.Q.I.* 1, 1888, 166-73.

Acomb
RICHARDSON, HAROLD, ed. *The parish register of Acomb, an ancient village of the West Riding of Yorkshire, now incorporated with the City of York. Vols. 1-10, 1663-1837 (bishops transcripts 1634-1760).* Y.P.R.S. 129. 1966.
'The records of the peculiar jurisdiction of Acomb', *B.I.B.* 2, 1979-82, 155-68. Includes marriage bonds, 1714-1863, and probate records 1456-1837.

Addingham
LUMB, GEORGE DENISON, ed. *The register of the parish church of Addingham, Co. York, 1612-1812.* Y.P.R.S. 129. 1920. Also available on fiche. For corrections and additions (from bishops' transcripts) for 1663-7, see:

CLAYTON, BRIAN. 'Addingham parish
registers', *Wh.N.* **24,** 1997, 14-15.
*Addingham St. Peter parish register:
marriage, burials, baptisms, 1813-1837.* 2
vols. Leeds: Wharfedale Family History
Group, 1998.
HARTLEY, JOHN, ed. *Wesleyan Methodist
baptisms, Addingham 1840-1899.
Draughton 1887-1899.* [ ]: Wharfedale
Family History Group, [1997].
CLAYTON, BRIAN, ed. *Addingham Wesleyan
Methodist marriages, 1843-1899.* [ ]:
Wharfedale Family History Group, [1997].
CLAYTON, BRIAN, ed. *Addingham Wesleyan
Methodist burials 1884-1995.* [ ]:
Wharfedale Family History Group [1997].

Adel

LUMB, GEORGE DENISON, ed. *The registers
of the parish church of Adel in the
County of York from 1606 to 1812, and
monumental inscriptions.* T.S. **5.** 1985.
LUMB, G.D. 'Adel register: transcript at York',
in *Miscellanea* **[6].** *T.S.* **2,** 1915, 107. For
1600 only.

Adlingfleet

Adlingfleet 1694-1972. Burial index **1.**
[Doncaster]: Doncaster & District F.H.S.,
1998.

Adwick le Street

Adwick le Street, St. Lawrence, 1547-1900.
Burial index **22.** Doncaster: Doncaster &
District F.H.S., [1999?]. Not seen.

Adwick upon Dearne

Adwick upon Dearne, 1690-1985. Burial
index **6.** Doncaster: Doncaster & District
F.H.S., 1998.

Aldborough

LAWSON-TANCRED, T., ed. *The parish register
of Aldborough (W.R.), vol. 1. 1538-1611.*
Y.P.R.S. **110.** 1940. Also available on fiche.

Allerton Mauleverer

SLINGSBY, F. WILLIAM, ed. *The registers of
the parish church of Allerton Mauleverer,
Co. York.* Y.P.R.S **31.** 1908. Marriages
1557-1753; baptisms 1562-1812; burials 1564-
1812.

Allertonshire

HOWE, JOHN J. 'Allertonshire marriage
bonds', *Northern genealogist* **1-4,** 1895-
1901, *passim.* For 1730-62.

Almondbury

TAYLOR, HARRY, ed. *The parish register of
Almondbury volume 1 (part 1). 1557-1598.*
Y.A.S., P.R.S. **139.** 1974.
TAYLOR, HARRY, ed. *The parish register of
Almondbury. Volume 1 (part 2). 1598-1652.*
Y.A.S., P.R.S. **140.** 1975.
TAYLOR, HARRY, & TAYLOR, JESSICA, eds.
*The parish register of Almondbury,
volume II. 1653-1682.* Y.A.S., P.R.S. **148.**
1984.
TAYLOR, HARRY, & TAYLOR, JESSICA, eds.
*The parish register of Almondbury,
volume 3. 1683-1703.* Y.A.S., P.R.S. **153.**
1988.

Arksey
See Bentley

Armley
See Holbeck and Leeds

Armthorpe

*Armthorpe, Saint Leonard and Saint Mary,
1654-1912.* Burial index **7.** Doncaster:
Doncaster & District F.H.S., 1998.

Arncliffe

SHUFFREY, WILLIAM ARTHUR, ed. *The
registers of the ancient parish of
Arncliffe including those of Halton Gill
and Hubberholme, 1663-1812.* Bradford:
G.F. Sewell, 1910. Includes extracts from
Paver's marriage licences, 1594-1640.

Askham Bryan

RICHARDSON, HAROLD, ed. *The parish
registers of Askham Bryan, vols 1-6, 1695-
1837 (bishops transcripts 1604-1694), and
Askham Richard, 1813-1837.* Y.P.R.S. **131.**
1967.

Askham Richard
See Askham Bryan

Atwick

CHARLESWORTH, JOHN, ed. *The parish
register of Atwick (E.R.) 1538-1708.*
Y.P.R.S. **111.** 1941. Also available on fiche.

Aughton
CHARLESWORTH, JOHN, ed. *The parish register of Aughton in the County of York.* Y.P.R.S. **86**. 1928. Also available on fiche. Covers 1610-1813, with marriages to 1825; includes list of parishioners, 1816.

Austerfield
LUMB, GEORGE DENISON, ed. *The registers of the chapel of Austerfield, in the parish of Blyth and in the County of York, 1559-1812.* Y.P.R.S. **39**. 1910.

Aysgarth
Bishops transcripts, Aysgath parish. Bishopdale booklets **5**. Bishopdale: Bishopdale Archives, 1993. Not seen.

Badsworth
LAZENBY, BRENDA, & BUCHANAN, SHARON. *St Mary parish church, Badsworth, in the West Riding of Yorkshire: marriage index, 1813-1837.* Pontefract: Pontefract & District F.H.S., [1998?]

Barnburgh
Barnburgh, 1558-1900. Burial index **4**. [Doncaster]: Doncaster & District F.H.S., 1998.

Barnby Dun
'Strays taken from Barnby Dun P.R., Yks', *Don. Anc.* 3(5), 1988, 155-6. 17-18th c.

Barnsley
ELLIOTT, BRIAN. 'Aspects of medical care in the Barnsley area during the seventeenth and eighteenth centuries', *O.W.R.* 6(1), 1986. 17-23. Includes extracts from Barnsley parish register, June-December 1777.

Barwick in Elmet
For registers 1653-1812, see section 3B below.

Batley
BELLINGHAM, ROGER A. 'Batley: another Dade register', *H.& D.F.H.S.J.* 8(2), 1995, 46-7. Discussion of the parish register made according to the 'Dade' format.

Beeston
'Beeston church parochial magazine, no. 1, January 1908, vol. 23', *Y.A.S., F.H.P.S.S.N.* 2(4), 1975 50-52. Baptisms, marriages and burials, 1906-8.
See also Leeds

Bentham
CHIPPINDALL, W.H., ed. *The parish register of Bentham (1666-1812).* Y.P.R.S. **91**. 1932. Also available on fiche.

Bentley
Cemetery burial registers: Bentley with Arksey Cemetery, 1885-1990. 7 fiche. Doncaster: Doncaster & District F.H.S., [199-?]. Not seen.

Bingley
STAVERT, W.J., ed. *The parish register of Bingley in the county of York, 1577-1686.* Y.P.R.S. **9**. 1901. Also available on fiche.
JONES, BRIAN, ed. *Bingley All Saints marriages, 1687-1720.* Bradford: Brian Jones, 1998.

Birstall
NUSSEY, JOHN, ed. *The parish register of Birstall. Volume 1. 1558-1635.* Y.A.S., P.R.S. **146**. 1983. Includes 'lists of rectors, vicars and churchwardens', with map of the parish.
NUSSEY, JOHN, ed. *The parish register of Birstall. Volume 2. 1636-1687.* Y.A.S., P.R.S. **152**. 1987.
'Birstall parish registers', *Y.G.* **1**, 1888, 25-8. Brief extracts.
THWAITE, HARTLEY. 'Birstall parish registers 1558-1837 (31 vols., 100 000 entries)', *Y.A.S., F.H.P.S.S.N.* 2(1), 1975, 6-10. General discussion.
See also Tong

Bishopthorpe
BRUNSKILL, ELIZABETH, ed. *The parish register of Bishopthorpe, 1631-1837.* Y.A.S., P.R.S. **150**. 1986.

Blacktoft
WEDDALL, GEORGE EDWARD, ed. *The registers of the parish church of Blacktoft, East Yorkshire, 1700-1812.* Y.P.R.S. **8**. 1900. Also available on fiche. Includes 5 entries from the bishop's transcript for 1639. Bound with WINN, ARTHUR T., ed. *The registers of Scorborough, co. of York,* which covers 1653-1803.

Bolton Abbey

CLAYTON, BRIAN, ed. *Bolton Abbey parish registers: some earlier years prior to 1689.* [ ]: Wharfedale Family History Group, 1997.

HOWES, A.P. *The parish register of Bolton Abbey, 1689 to 1812.* Skipton: Craven Herald, 1895.

Bolton Abbey parish registers, 1689-1812. Leeds: Wharfedale Family History Group, [199-?]. Not seen.

Bolton Abbey parish registers, 1813 to 1837: transcription and index on microfiche. Booklet + 1 fiche. [ ]: Wharfedale Family History Group, 1993.

Bolton by Bowland

STAVERT, W.J., ed. *The parish register of Bolton-by-Bolland in the County of York, 1558-1724.* Y.P.R.S. 19. 1904. Also available on fiche.

STAVERT, W.J., ed. *The parish register of Bolton-by-Bowland in the County of York, 1725-1812.* Y.P.R.S. 22. 1905. 'Part II' on cover. Also available on fiche.

Lancashire marriage index: Bolton-by-Bowland, 1813-37 (by grooms & bride). B14. 1 fiche. Sale: Rossendale Society for Genealogy, Heraldry and Lancashire, 1983.

Boroughbridge Deanery

See Richmondshire

Bowes

ALDERSON, BASIL ROXBY, ed. *The parish register of Bowes, 1670-1837 (bishops transcripts 1615-1700).* Y.A.S., P.R.S. 127. 1964. Includes list of pew holders, 1703, lists of local schools and wills, *etc.* Also available on fiche.

GARDNER, SUSAN. 'Burial of boys in the delightful village of Dotheboys', *J.Cl.F.H.S.* 6(3), 1995, 41-2. Actually, list of pupils of various schools buried at Bowes, from the parish register, 1810-34.

Bradfield

BROWNE, ARTHUR BRIARLY, ed. *Registers of Bradfield in the Diocese of York, 1559-1722.* Sheffield: A. MacDougall and Sons, 1905.

Bradford

EMPSALL, T.W. 'Copy of buriall register of Bradford parish church', *B.A.* 1, 1888, 46-50, 102-6, 160-64, 227-32 & 285-8; 2, 1895, 1-8, 111-16, 156-61, 192-7 & 271-6; N.S., 1, 1900, 67-80, 159-68, 313-24, 403-14, & 515-26; N.S., 2, 1905, 56-67, 152-63, 300-307 & 511-22; 3, 1912, 68-77. 1596-1680.

Bradford parish church: marriages, 1596-1615. Bradford: Brian Jones, 1998. Reprinted from *B.A.*

Bradford parish church: burials, 1596-1605. Keighley: Brian Jones, 1997. Reprinted from *B.A.*

Bradford parish church: burials, 1606-1615. Bradford: Brian Jones, 1998. Reprinted from *B.A.*

BRADFORD FAMILY HISTORY SOCIETY. *Name Index To Bradford parish church burial registers, 1681-1837.* 6 vols. Bradford F.H.S., 1997. Also available on 12 fiche.

Kirkgate

JONES, BRIAN. *Bradford. Kirkgate Wesleyan Chapel: baptisms 1820-1837.* Bradford: Brian Jones, 1998.

Sion Chapel, Bridge Street

JONES, BRIAN. *Sion Chapel, Bridge Street, Bradford: register book of births, and supplementary book, 1814-1837.* Bradford: Brian Jones, 1996.

Toad Lane Chapel

JONES, BRIAN. *Toad Lane Chapel, Bradford. Baptisms 1730 to 1756.* Bradford: Brian Jones, 1997.

Braithwell

TILLOTT, P.M., ed. *The parish register of Braithwell, volume 1. 1559-1774.* Y.A.S., P.R.S. 132. 1969. Includes terrier, 1559, will of John Gleadale, 1688, and notes on John Bosvile's charity, 18th c.

TILLOTT, P.M., ed. *The parish register of Braithwell, vols. II, III, IV, V and VI, 1754-1837.* Y.A.S., P.R.S. 133. 1969. Includes list of incumbents, terriers of 1786 and 1905, will of Margaret Sheppard, 1864, *etc.*

Bramley

See Leeds

Brampton Bierlow
Brampton Bierlow, 1855-1911. Burial index **2.** [Doncaster]: Doncaster & District F.H.S., 1998.

Brandesburton
HICKS, J.D., ed. *The parish register of Brandsburton, 1558- 1837.* Y.A.S., P.R.S. **142.** 1979. Includes list of rectors, 1251-1958.

Brantingham
WEDDALL, GEORGE EDWARD, ed. *The registers of the parish church of Brantingham, East Yorkshire, 1653-1812.* Y.P.R.S. **12.** 1902. Also available on fiche.

Bridlington Priory
Baptisms solemnised in the parish of Bridlington Priory in the County of York, March 1782 to December 1812. Cottingham: E.Y.F.H.S., 1996.
Bridlington Priory: baptisms, 1813 to 1837. Cottingham: E.Y.F.H.S., 1990.
Bridlington Priory: marriages, 1813 to 1837. [ ]: E.Y.F.H.S., 1991.
Burials in the parish of Bridlington Priory, in the County of York, March 1782 to December 1812. Cottingham: E.Y.F.H.S., 1997.
Bridlington Priory: burials, 1813 to 1837. [ ]: E.Y.F.H.S., 1993.

Brodsworth
WHITING, C.E., ed. *The parish register of Brodsworth, 1538- 1813.* Y.P.R.S. **104.** 1937. Also available on fiche.

Bubwith
CHARLESWORTH, JOHN, ed. *The parish register of Bubwith: baptism and burials 1600-1767; marriages 1600-1753. Part 1.* Y.P.R.S. **99.** 1935.

Bulmer
WILSON, ELLEN, ed. *The parish register of Bulmer, 1571-1837.* Y.A.S., P.R.S. **160.** 1995.

Burghwallis
WHITING, C.E., ed. *The parish register of Burghwallis, Yorks: baptisms 1596-1814, marriages 1596-1814; burials 1596-1810.* Y.P.R.S. **116.** 1945.
Burghwallis St. Helen 1597-1955. Burial index **5.** [Doncaster]: Doncaster & District F.H.S., 1998.

Burnsall
STAVERT, W.J., ed. *The parish register of Burnsall-in-Craven, 1559-1700.* Skipton: Craven Herald, 1893.
STAVERT, W.J., ed. *The parish register of Burnsall-in-Craven, 1701-1739, 1783-1812.* Skipton: Craven Herald Office, 1893.
STAVERT, W.J., ed. *The parish register of Burnsall-in-Craven 1813-1900.* Skipton: Craven Herald, 1915.
STAVERT, W.J., ed. *The parish register of Burnsall-in-Craven: missing portions recovered from the transcripts at York, together with the more ancient inscriptions on monuments in the church and churchyard, entries of the marriages of Burnsall folk in other registers, and such as refer to them in Paver's licences, some notes of the rectors and other clergy who have ministered in the parish.* Skipton: Craven Herald Office, 1912.
See also Conistone and Rylstone

Burton Fleming
PARK, G.E., & LUMB, G.D., eds. *The register of the parish church of Burton Fleming, otherwise North Burton, 1538-1812.* Y.P.R.S. **2.** 1899. Also available on fiche.

Burton Salmon
Baptisms solemized in Wesleyan Methodist Chapel, Burton Salmon, 1872-1985. Pontefract: Pontefract & District F.H.S., 1999. Not seen.

Calverley
MARGERISON, SAMUEL, ed. *The first volume of the registers of the parish church of Calverley, in the West Riding of the County of York, with a description of the church, and a sketch of its history prior to 1650.* Bradford: G.F. Sewell, 1880. Includes baptisms 1681-1720, marriages, 1681-1720 and burials, 1681-1720; also notes from wills, register of seats, 1606, *etc.*
MARGERISON, SAMUEL, ed. *The registers of the parish church of Calverley, in the West Riding of the County of Yorkshire, with a description of the church and a sketch of its history. Volume II.* Bradford: G.F. Sewell, 1883. Baptisms 1670-79; marriages 1649-80; burials 1649-80. Also includes monumental inscriptions, list of churchwardens, *etc.*

MARGERISON, SAMUEL, ed. *The registers of the parish church of Calverley, in the West Riding of the County of York, with a description of the church and a sketch of its history. Volume III. Containing the registers from 1681 to 1720, with notes.* Bradford: G.F. Sewell, 1887. Includes notes from wills, *etc.*

Campsall
Campsall, St. Mary Magdalene, 1563-1716. 2 vols. Burial index **10-11.** Doncaster: Doncaster & District F.H.S., 1998. Not seen.
Campsall, St. Mary Magdalene, 1717-1900. Burial index **12-13.** Doncaster: Doncaster & District F.H.S., [1998?]

Cantley
WHITING, C.E., ed. *The parish register of Cantley, 1539- 1812.* Y.P.R.S. **112.** 1941.

Carlton
KAYE, WALTER J., ed. *The parish register of Carlton-juxta-Snaith (1598-1812).* Y.P.R.S. **96.** 1933.

Castleford
LAZENBY, BRENDA. *All Saints parish church, Castleford, in the West Riding of Yorkshire: marriage index, 1813-1837.* Pontefract: Pontfract & District F.H.S., 1998.

Catterick Deanery
See Richmondshire

Chapel Allerton
See Leeds

Chapel le Dale
See Ingleton

Cherry Burton
WINN, ARTHUR T., ed. *The registers of the parish church of Cherry Burton, Co. York, 1561-1740.* Y.P.R.S. **15.** 1903. Also available on fiche.

Clapham
CHARLESWORTH, JOHN, ed. *The parish register of Clapham, Co. York. Part 1. 1595-1683.* Y.P.R.S. **67.** 1921. Also available on fiche.

Clayton
See Frickley

Collingham
EXWOOD, ELISABETH, ed. *The parish register of Collingham, 1579-1837.* Y.A.S., P.R.S. **141.** 1978.

Conisbrough
Cemetery burial registers: Conisbrough Cemetery, 1900-1951. 12 fiche. Doncaster: Doncaster & District F.H.S., [199-?]. Not seen.

Conistone
STAVERT, W.J., ed. *The register of St. Mary's Chapel at Conistone, in the parish of Burnsall-in-Craven, 1567-1812.* Skipton: Craven Herald, 1894.

Copgrove
MAJOR, HENRY D. *Memorials of Copgrove, together with the parish registers from A.D.1584 to 1790.* Oxford: Basil Blackwell, 1922.

Copmanthorpe
HARBIDGE, JOHN, ed. *The parish registers of St. Giles, Copmanthorpe, York, 1759-1837.* York F.H.S. publications 3. 1979.

Cotherstone
BELL, GEORGE, & YELLOWLEY, CAROL. *Cotherstone Particular Meeting Quaker records 1588-1992;* Wideopen: Original Indexes, 1997. Births, 1588-1843; marriages, 1647-1859; deaths, 1657-1852; interments, 1797-1896; monumental inscriptions, 1822-1922.

Cowick
Cowick, Holy Trinity, 1854-1970. Burial index **20.** Doncaster: Doncaster & District F.H.S., [1999?]. Not seen.

Coxwold
LLOYD, R.L.H., ed. *The parish registers of Coxwold (part 1): 1583-1666.* Y.P.R.S. **120.** 1955. Also available on fiche.

Crofton
TOWNEND, WILLIAM, ed. *The parish registers of Crofton, Co. York, 1615-1812.* Y.P.R.S. **62.** 1918. Also available on fiche.

Cundall

ESHELBY, HENRY D., ed. *The parish register of Cundall with Norton-le-Clay, in the North Riding of the County of York, 1582 to 1780.* Birkenhead: privately printed, 1898.

Danby in Cleveland

COLLINS, F., ed. *The registers of Danby-in-Cleveland, 1585 to 1812.* Y.P.R.S. **43.** 1912. Also available on fiche.

HANSOM, JOSEPH S., ed. 'Catholic registers of Danby, West Witton, and Leyburn, Yorkshire, 1742-1840, with notes of the Scrope family, 1663-1754', in *Miscellanea* 8. C.R.S., **13,** 1913, 227-87.

Darfield

S., J. 'A Yorkshire private burial record', *Y.C.M.* **1,** 1891, 146-57. List of the deaths of friends of Elkanah Piggott of Darfield, 1755-1811.

Darrington

LUMB, GEORGE DENISON, ed. *The register of the parish church of Darrington, Co. York, 1567-1812.* Y.P.R.S., **49.** 1913.

LAZENBY, BRENDA. *St. Luke's parish church, Darrington, in the West Riding of Yorkshire: marriage index 1813-1837.* Pontefract: Pontefract & District F.H.S., 1998.

MORTON, DAVE. *St. Luke's parish church, Darrington, in the West Riding of Yorkshire: burial index 1813-1881 (Feb).* Pontfract: Pontefract & District F.H.S., 1998.

Dent

KENDALL, WM. CLEMENT. 'Notes from the parish register of Dent', *Northern genealogist* **5,** 1902, 88-9. Brief extracts.

Dewsbury

CHADWICK, SAMUEL JOSEPH, ed. *The registers of Dewsbury, Yorkshire. Vol. 1. 1538 to 1653.* Dewsbury: Joseph Ward & Co., [1898].

Doncaster

BLUMHARDT, E.K., ed. *Yorkshire marriage registers, West Riding, vol. III[-IV]: Doncaster.* 2 vols. Philimore's parish register series, **218-9.** Phillimore & Co., 1915. Pt. 1. 1557-1784. Pt. 2. 1785-1837. Many errors.

MACQUIBAN, TIM. 'Extracts from a talk on nonconformist records', *Don. Anc.* **2**(1), 1983, 13-16. Includes list of Doncaster Circuit Methodist registers.

'Doncaster Metropolitan Borough Archives Department: Cemetery records', *Islonian* **2**(6), 1990, 23.

Draughton

See Addingham, and section 2B below

Drypool

INGRAM, M. EDWARD, ed. *The parish register of Drypool, vols 1-5. Baptisms and burials 1572-1812; marriages 1572-1807.* Y.P.R.S. **125.** 1961. Also available on fiche.

BOULTER, W. CONSITT. 'Some extracts from the parish registers of Drypool, in the East Riding of Yorkshire', *Reliquary* **10,** 1869-70, 54-9; **11,** 1870-71, 88-91. For 1572-1803.

Easingwold

LUMB, GEORGE DENISON, ed. *The register of the parish church of All Saints, Easingwold, Co. York, 1599-1812.* Y.P.R.S., **56.** 1916. Also available on fiche.

GURNEY, NORAH K.M., et al, *The parish registers of Easingwold, Raskelf and Myton upon Swale, 1813-1837.* Y.A.S., P.R.S. **145.** 1983.

East Rounton

ROBSON, WILLIAM THOMAS, ed. *The register of the chapelry of East Rounton in the parish of Rudby-in-Cleveland, Co. York, 1595- 1837.* Y.P.R.S. **54.** 1916. Also available on fiche.

Ecclesfield

GATTY, ALFRED SCOTT, ed. *The first book of the marriage, baptismal, and burial registers of Ecclesfield parish church, Yorkshire from 1558 to 1619; also the churchwardens' accounts from 1520 to 1546.* Bell & Sons, 1878.

Elland

CLAY, JOHN WILLIAM, ed. *The registers of Elland, Co. Yorkshire, Vol. 1. 1559 to 1640.* Leeds: J. Whitehead & Son, [1897].

ORMEROD, H., ed. *The parish registers of Elland, Co. York, 1640-1670, & churchwardens' accounts, 1648-1670, etc.* Oxford: B.H. Blackwell, 1917. Includes list of churchwardens, 1576-1761, of 'cantarists, curates and rectors of Elland', 14-19th c., and seating list, 1583.

ORMEROD, H., ed. *The parish registers of Elland, Co. York, 1671 to 1714, etc.* Oxford: B.H.Blackwell, 1925. Includes seating list, 1583, extracts from churchwardens' accounts, 1671-2, subscription list 1690, *etc*. 'The Elland registers', *Scrivenor* **79**, 1997, 33-8. General discussion.

Elvington
'Elvington', *B.T.* **30**, 1987, 14-17. Includes baptisms marriages and burials printed in the Elvington *Monthly paper* for 1870.

Emley
CHARLESWORTH, JOHN, ed. *The parish register of Emley, Co. York: baptisms, marriages and burials, 1600 to 1812*. Y.P.R.S. **65**. 1921.

CHARLESWORTH, JOHN, ed. *The parish register of Emley, Co. York: baptisms, marriages and burials, 1813-1836. Vol. II.* Wakefield: Sanderson & Clayton, 1921.

Eston
KAYE, WALTER J., ed. *The parish register of Eston (1590- 1812).* Y.P.R.S. **76**. 1924. Also available on fiche.

Etton
HICKS, J.D. *The parish registers of Etton, East Yorkshire, 1654-1837.* [ ], 1994.

Everingham Park
HANSOM, JOSEPH STANISLAUS, ed. 'Catholic registers of St. Mary's domestic chapel, Everingham Park, Yorkshire, with historical notes', in *Miscellanea* **6**. C.R.S. **7**, 1909, 260-95.

Farnham
COLLINS, FRANCIS, ed. *The registers of Farnham, Yorkshire, 1569-1812.* Parish Register Society **56**. 1905.

Farnley
See Leeds

Featherstone
All Saints, Featherstone, in the West Riding of Yorkshire. Marriage index, 1813-1837. Pontefreact: Pontefract & District F.H.S., 1998.

Felkirk
ROYDS, A. NORA J., ed. *The registers of the parish church of Felkirk in the Diocese and county of York, from May 1701 to December 1812.* Rochdale: James Clegg, 1894. Includes list of vicars, various terriers, *etc*.

LAZENBY, BRENDA. *St. Peter parish church, Felkirk, in the West Riding of Yorkshire: marriage index 1754-1812.* Pontefract: Pontefract & District F.H.S., [1998?].

BRISCOE, GILL. *St Peter parish church, Felkirk, in the West Riding of Yorkshire: marriage index 1813-1837.* Pontefract: Pontefract & District F.H.S., [1998?]

ARNOLD, HILARY. 'Felkirk parish register transcriptions', *Barnsley F.H.S. newsletter.* July 1992, 14-15. Brief notes on the author's transcript.

Fewston
PARKINSON, THOMAS, ed. *The registers of the parish church (St Michael and All Angels) of Fewston, in the county of York, A.D. 1593 to A.D. 1812.* 2 vols. Skipton: Craven Herald Office, 1899. Vol. 1. 1593-1723. Vol. 2. 1723-1812.

Flockton
See Thornhill

Frickley cum Clayton
WHITING, C.E., ed. *The parish register of Frickley-with-Clayton (1577-1812).* Y.P.R.S. **95**. 1933. Also available on fiche.

Garforth
LUMB, GEORGE DENISON, ed. *The register of the parish church of Garforth, Co. York, 1631-1812.* Y.P.R.S. **46**. 1913. Also available on fiche.

Gargrave
STAVERT, W.J., ed. *The parish register of Gargrave in the County of York, 1558-1812.* Y.P.R.S. **28**. 1907. Also available on fiche.

Garsdale
BREAY, JOHN, ed. *The Quaker registers of Ravenstonedale, Grisedale and Garsdale, 1650-1837, with the second register of Birks Chapel, Warcop, 1754-1837, and extracts from the life of Stephen Brunskill of Orton (1748-1836), Methodist preacher.* Sedbergh: R.F.G. Hallett & Son, 1994. Quaker births, marriages and burials on the Westmorland border (Garsdale is in Yorkshire).

Giggleswick
HOYLE, R.W., ed. *The parish register of Giggleswick. Volume 1. 1558-1669.* Y.A.S., P.R.S. **147**. 1984.
HOYLE, R.W., ed. *The parish register of Giggleswick. Volume 2. 1669-1769.* Y.A.S., P.R.S. **151**. 1986.
Hoyle's work supersedes the inaccurate:
FOSTER, JOHN, ed. *The registers of the ancient parish church of Giggleswick-in-Craven, Yorkshire.* Settle: Caxton Press, [1906?] Covers 1558-1605.

Gilling
HUDSON, E.C., ed. *The parish register of Gilling, York, 1573- 1812.* Y.P.R.S. **113**. 1942. Also available on fiche.
HUDSON, E.C. 'A Yorkshire country parish, 1676-1710', *Y.A.J.* **36**, 1944-7, 116-25. Extracts from Gilling parish register.

Gisborough Priory
P. 'Extracts from a volume of Robert Aske's collections, marked with a cinquefoil, written in the reign of Henry VIII', *Collectanea topographica et genealogica* **1**, 1834, 168-70. Includes list of medieval burials at Gisborough Priory.

Gisburn
SIMPSON, STEPHEN, & CHARLESWORTH, JNO., eds. *The parish register of Gisburne (part I), Yorks., 1558-1745.* Y.P.R.S. **114**. 1943. Also available on fiche. Includes list of rectors, 13-20th c.
LONG, A.E., ed. *The parish register of Gisburne (part II), Yorks., 1745-1812.* Y.P.R.S. **118**. 1952. Also available on fiche.

Givendale
'Givendale register transcripts', *Northern genealogist* **3**, 1900, 130-31. For 1699-1710.

Great Ayton
KAYE, WALTER J., ed. *The parish register of Great Ayton (1600-1812).* Y.P.R.S. **90**. 1931. Also available on fiche.

Great Horton
JONES, BRIAN, ed. *Great Horton Primitive Methodist chapel, Bradford: baptisms 1824-1837; burials, 1825-1837.* Keighley: Brian Jones, 1997.

JONES, BRIAN. *Great Horton Wesleyan Chapel, Bradford: baptisms 1816 to 1837.* Keighley: Brian Jones, 1997.

Greenhow Hill
See below, section 2B, for burial register, 1855-1996.

Grindleton
HULL, NORAH, HULL, ROLAND, & HORNBY, DOREEN. eds. *Register of burials in the Chapelry of Grindleton, in the county of York, January 9th 1813 to January 9th 1924.* **G8**. 2 fiche. [ ]: Lancashire Family History and Heraldry Society, 1991.

Grinton in Swaledale
SLINGSBY, F. WILLIAM, ed. *The registers of the parish church of Grinton in Swaledale, Co. York.* Y.P.R.S. **23**. 1905. Also available on fiche. Baptisms and burials, 1640-1807; marriages 1640-1802.
See also Scarborough

Guiseley
PRESTON, WILLIAM EASTERBROOK, & ROWE, JOSEPH HAMBLEY, eds. *A transcript of the early registers of the parish of Guiseley in the county of York, 1584 to 1720, together with a transcript of the early registers of the chapelry of Horsforth 1620 to 1720, with notes on Guiseley families.* Bradford: Percy Lund Humphries & Co., 1913. Includes extracts from various other parochial documents, and notes on local families.
CLELLAND, MRS. 'Strays', *Y.A.S., F.H.P.S.S.N.* **10**(3), 1984, 169-70. From Guiseley bishops' transcripts, 1782-1823.

Hackness
JOHNSTONE, CHARLES, & HART, EMILY J., eds. *The register of the parish of Hackness, Co. York, 1557-1783.* Y.P.R.S. **25**. 1906. Also available on fiche.
SEDMAN, G. 'Mingle not truth and falsehood', *Family tree magazine* **10**(1), 1993 27-8. Brief extracts from, and discussion of, the Hackness parish register 1636-59.

Halifax
CROSSLEY, E.W., ed. *The parish registers of Halifax, Co. York. Vol. I. Baptisms, 1538 to 1593.* Y.P.R.S. **37**. 1910. Also available on fiche.

CROSSLEY, E.W., ed. *The parish registers of Halifax, Co. York. Vol. II. Marriages and burials, 1538-1593.* Y.P.R.S. **45**. 1912. Reprinted Bowie, Maryland: Heritage Books, 1995. Also available on fiche.

WALKER, WALTER JAMES. *Chapters on the early registers of Halifax parish church.* Halifax: Whitley & Booth, 1885. Extensive discussion with many extracts from the parish register.

SLACK, MARGARET. 'Non-conformist and Anglican registration in the Halifax area, 1740-99', *Local population studies* **38**, 1987, 44-5. Brief note with statistics of baptisms and burials.

'Halifax parish church registers', *Y.N.Q.I.* **2**, 1890, 318-22. Abstract for 1541-2.

'Halifax parish church registers', *Y.C.M.* **1**, 1891, 55-6, 123-7, 220-23 & 257-60. For 1542-5.

'Halifax parish register (continued)', *Y.C.M.* **4**, 1894, 162-5. 1544 burials, plus brief extracts to 1593.

Papers read to the annual meeting of 'Friends', 1938. [Halifax]: Society of Friends of Halifax Parish Church, 1938. Contents: HANSON, T.W. 'The ancient parish of Halifax. CROSSLEY, E.W. *The Halifax parish registers.* Brief essays.

Halton Gill
See Arncliffe

Hampsthwaite
COLLINS, FRANCIS, ed. *The registers of Hampsthwaite, Co. York. Marriages 1603-1807; baptisms 1603-1794; burials 1603-1794.* Y.P.R.S. **13**. 1902. Also available on fiche.

Harewood
BRIGG, WILLIAM, ed. *The parish registers of Harewood, Co. York. Part I: baptisms, 1614 to 1812; marriages 1621 to 1812.* Y.P.R.S. **50**. 1914. Also available on fiche.

Harrogate
KAYE, WALTER J. *Records of Harrogate, including the register of Christ Church (1748-1812), with supplementary extracts from Knaresborough (1560-1753), notes on the pre-Reformation chantry and the early history of the waters, early inhabitants, and extracts from the parish accounts of Pannal, Knaresborough and Clint, and from court rolls, quarter sessions rolls and muster rolls.* Leeds: F.J. Walker, 1922.

Hartshead
ARMYTAGE, EDITH B., ed. *The parish register of Hartshead in the County of York, 1612-1812.* Y.P.R.S. **17**. 1903. Also available on fiche.

Hatfield
BROWN, BEN. 'The Hatfield sexton's day book', *Don. Anc.* **3**(2), 1986, 52-3. Brief description of a late 19th c. listing of graves dug.

Hawnby
'The register booke for the parish of Hawnsby, Yorke', *Y.C.M.* **3**, 1893, 153-68 & 201-16; **4**, 1894, 12-23. 1654-1722.

Haworth
'Marriages at Haworth', *K.D.F.H.S.J.* Autumn 1998- , *passim.* To 1812 (listed in date order, backwards). To be continued.

'Stanbury Quaker register (Haworth)', *Y.N.Q.I.* **1**, 1888, 9-15. See also **2**, 1880, 231-2. Includes burials, 1656-1718, a few marriages and births, *etc.*

Headingley
See Leeds

Hedon
CRAVEN, MARTIN, ed. *The Hedon parish registers.* 2 vols. Beverley: Highgate Publications, 1993. v.1. Baptisms 1552-1885; marriages 1552-1881; burials 1549-1893. v.2. Baptisms 1552-1885; marriages 1552-1881; burials 1549-1893.
See also Nut Hill

Hemsworth
CHARLESWORTH, JOHN, ed. *The register of the parish of Hemsworth, Co. York 1654-1812.* Y.P.R.S. **79**. 1926. Alternative title: *The parish register of Hemsworth in the County of York.*

BRISCOE, GILL. *St. Helen's parish church, Hemsworth, in the West Riding of Yorkshire: marriage index, 1813-1837.* Pontefract: Pontefract & District F.H.S., 1998.

Heptonstall
HORSFALL, EDITH, ed. *The parish registers of Heptonstall, in the County of York. Vol. 1. 1593-1660, containing baptisms July 8, 1599-Sept 2, 1660; marriages, Jan 2, 1593-Sept 2, 1653. Jan 14 1657-Aug. 28, 1660; burials, Jan 12, 1593-Sept 16, 1653.* Y.P.R.S. **78**. 1925. Also available on fiche.

OGDEN, ARTHUR. 'The Heptonstall church registers', *P.R.H.A.S.* 1908, 157-73. Discussion with some abstracts.

Heslington

SMITH, MARGARET E., ed. *The parish register of Heslington, 1639-1837.* Y.A.S., P.R.S. 1982.

Hickleton

WHITING, C.E., ed. *The parish register of St Wilfred's, Hickleton, 1626-1812.* Y.P.R.S. **109**. 1940. Includes terriers, 18th c.

Holbeck

LUMB, GEORGE DENISON, ed. *The registers of the chapels of the parish church of Leeds from 1764 to 1812: Holbeck, Armley, and Hunslet.* T.S. **31**. 1934.
See also Leeds

Holme upon Spalding Moor

HANSOM, JOSEPH S., ed. 'The Catholic registers of Holme-on-Spalding Moor, E.R. of York', in *Miscellanea* **4**. C.R.S. **4**. 1907, 272-318.

Holmfirth

WOODCOCK, MARGARET, et al. 'Found dead, Fifth February 1852, at Wooldale', *H.& D.F.H.S.J.* **4**(2), 1991, 48-9. Includes list of fatalities in the Holmfirth flood of 1852.

Holmpton

PATTINSON, P.M., ed. *Holmpton: marriages 1739-1837.* East Riding transcripts **2**. Willerby: E.Y.F.H.S., [198-].

Honley

WALKER, RITA. 'Burials in the garden of rest, Honley', *H. & D.F.H.S.J.* **10**(1), 1996, 30. List of burials in the 1970s and 1980s.

Hooton Pagnell

WHITING, C.E., ed. *The parish registers of Hooton Pagnell (1538-1812).* Y.P.R.S. **87**. 1929. Also available on fiche.

Horbury

CHARLESWORTH, JOHN, ed. *The registers of the chapel of Horbury, in the parish of Wakefield in the County of York, 1598-1812.* Y.P.R.S. **3**. 1900.

Horsforth

See Guiseley

Horton

'Quaker Lane burial ground, Horton', *Bodkin* **8**, 1987, 17. List of interments, 1656-99.

Howden

WEDDALL, G.E., ed. *The registers of Howden, Co. York. Vol. 1. (1543-1659).* Y.P.R.S. **21**. 1904.

WEDDALL, G.E., ed. *The registers of the parish of Howden, Co. York. Vol. II. (1543-1702).* Y.P.R.S. **24**. 1905.

WEDDALL, G.E., ed. *The registers of the parish of Howden, Co. York. Vol. II (Continued).* Y.P.R.S. **32**. 1908. 'Part III' on cover. Burials 1659-1723; marriages 1703-25 and 1743; baptisms 1703-25.

WEDDALL, G.E., ed. *The parish registers of Howden, 1725-1770.* Y.P.R.S. **48**. 1913.

Hubberholme

See Arncliffe

Huddersfield

WHITWAM, STEPHEN D., ed. *Huddersfield parish church: baptisms 1750-1759.* Huddersfield: H. & D.F.H.S., 1989. Index only. Further volumes cover 1760-1770 (1990), 1771-1778 (1991), 1793-1798 (1991), 1799-1805 (1988) and 1813-1819 (1990).

WHITWAM, STEPHEN DAVID, ed. *Huddersfield parish church: marriages, 1690-1724.* Huddersfield: H. & D.F.H.S., 1992. A further volume covers 1724-1756. (1989).

TOMLINSON, G.W. 'Extracts from the Huddersfield registers', *M.G.H.* 2nd series **2**, 1888, 382-4. 16th c.

GRUNDY, JOAN. 'Exhumations of Queen Street Chapel, Huddersfield', *H. & D.F.H.S.J.* **6**(4), 1993, 130-32. Includes list of burials, 1819-55.

Huddersfield High Street Methodist Church: baptisms, 1794- 1815. Huddersfield: H. & D.F.H.S., 1990.

Huggate

HOBDAY, EDITH, ed. *The registers of Huggate, Yorkshire, 1539- 1812.* Parish Register Society **36**. 1901. Includes list of clergy.

OLLARD, S.L. 'A recently discovered parish register', *Y.A.J.* **26**, 1922, 309-25. Discussion of a 17th c. volume of the Huggate register, which includes many entries not in the printed register.

Hull

Bowl Alley Lane

Dissenting (Unitarian) Bowl Alley Lane Chapel, Hull: register of baptisms, 1705-1837. [Hull]: privately published, [199-.]

Charterhouse

CAWLEY, A.P.D. 'Extracts from the register of marriages at the Charterhouse, Hull', *B.T.* **13**, 1982, 4-5. 1695-1714.

Holy Trinity

SYKES, JOHN. 'Extracts from the registers of the church of Holy Trinity, Hull', *Y.A.J.* **14**, 1896-7, 185-219.

St. Mary's

SYKES, JOHN. 'St Mary's, Hull', *Y.A.J.* **12**, 1893, 464-80. Extracts from the burial register 1569-1785.

Hunslet

See Holbeck and Leeds

Idle

HALL, AUDREY. 'Ebenezer Primitive Methodist Church, Idle, Bradford: baptismal register, Sept. 1826-Dec. 1900', *Bod-kin* **34**, 1994, 4. List of surnames only.

HALL, AUDREY. 'Thorp (Wesleyan) Methodist Church, Idle, baptism register 1811-1860', *Bod-kin* **31**, 1993, 3. List of surnames only.

Ilkley

COOPER, WILLIAM, ed. *The parish register of Ilkley (1597-1812).* Y.P.R.S. **83**. 1927. Also available on fiche.

BOYD, HUGH F. 'Extracts from the parish register of Ilkley, in the County of Yorkshire, and Deanery of Craven', *M.G.H.* N.S., **3**, 1880, 116-8. 1599-1654. Not continued.

'Miscellaneous gleanings from Ilkley parish registers', *K.D.F.H.S.J.* Summer 1995, 8-9. 18-19th c. extracts.

Ingleby Greenhow

The register booke of Ingleby iuxta Grenhow as much as is extant in the old booke for christenings, weddings and burials since the year of our Lord 1539 by me John Blackburne, curate. Canterbury: Cross & Jackman, 1889. To 1800.

Ingleton

CHIPPINDALL, W.H., ed. *The parish registers of the churches of Ingleton and Chapel-le-Dale, 1607-1812.* Y.P.R.S. **94**. 1933. Jointly published with the Lancashire Parish Register Society (v. 71.) Includes list of officiating clergy. Also available on fiche.

Keighley

BRIGG, WM. ANDERTON, ed. *The parish registers of St. Andrew's, Keighley. Vol. I: baptisms, marriages and burials April 1562-September 1649.* Y.P.R.S. **77**. 1925. Also available on fiche.

BRIGG, WM. ANDERTON, ed. *The parish registers of St. Andrew's, Keighley. Vol. II: baptisms, marriages and burials October 1649-March 1688.* Y.P.R.S. **82**. 1927. Also available on fiche.

LIVETT, RONALD G.C., ed. *The parish registers of St. Andrew's, Keighley, part III: baptisms, marriages and burials, March 1689-March 1735/6.* Y.P.R.S. **98**. 1935. Also available on fiche.

Register of strays: Keighley and district immigrants. 2 vols. Keighley Family History Publications, 1995-7.

Baptist Chapel

ROBINSON, D. 'Interments at Keighley Baptist Chapel yard, Turkey Street, from the burial register', *K.D.F.H.S.J.* Winter 1992, 23-4. Early 19th c.

Society of Friends

Register of births, marriages, deaths and burials of the Society of Friends at Keighley, West Yorkshire, 17th to 20th centuries. Keighley: Keighley Family History Publishing, 1997.

'Keighley Quaker register', *Y.N.Q.I.* **2**, 1890, 87-96, 145- 160 & 225-31. Births 1654-1765; marriages 1661-1772; deaths 1658-1845.

Kellington

BRISCOE, GILL. *St. Edmund, King & Martyr, parish church, Kellington, in the West Riding of Yorkshire: marriage index 1813-1837.* Pontefract: Pontefract & District F.H.S., 1998.

Kettlewell

Kettlewell St Mary: an index of the parish registers, 1698-1760. Leeds: Wharfedale Family History Group, 1998.

Kilburn

LUMB, GEORGE DENISON, ed. *The registers of the parish church of Kilburn, Co. York, 1600-1812.* Y.P.R.S. **61**. 1918.

Kildwick

BRIGG, WM. ANDERTON, ed. *The parish registers of St. Andrew's, Kildwick in Craven. Vol. I. Baptisms, deaths and marriages, 1575-1622.* Y.P.R.S. **47**. 1913. Also available on fiche.

BRIGG, WM. ANDERTON, ed. *The parish registers of St. Andrew's, Kildwick in Craven, vols. II and III. Baptisms, marriages and burials April 1623-August 1678.* Y.P.R.S. **55**. 1916. Also available on fiche.

LIVETT, RONALD G.C., ed. *The parish registers of St. Andrew's, Kildwick in Craven, vols. IV, V, and VI. Baptisms, marriages and burials September 1678-March 1743.* Y.P.R.S. **69**. 1922. Also available on fiche.

LIVETT, RONALD G.C., ed. *The parish register of Kildwick in Craven, IV [vols VII and VIII (in part)]. Baptisms March 1744-April 1789; marriages March 1744-March 1754; burials March 1744-June 1771.* Y.P.R.S. **92**. 1932. Also available on fiche.

Kippax

LUMB, GEORGE DENISON, ed. *The registers of the parish church of Kippax, Co. York, 1539-1812.* Y.P.R.S. **10**. 1901. Also available on fiche.

Kipping

ROBERTSHAW, WILFRED, ed. *Registers of the Independent chapel of Kipping in Thornton, parish of Bradford.* Bradford Historical and Antiquarian Society local record series **4**. 1953.

Kirby Grindalythe

'Kirby Grindalythe baptisms', *B.T.* **21**, 1985, 9-12. 1786-96. Also includes extracts from White's 1840 *directory*, and voters' list 1890.

Kirby Hill

BROWNE, A.B., & CHARLESWORTH, JOHN, eds. *The parish register of Kirby Hill (1576-1812).* Y.P.R.S. **75**. 1924. Includes terriers, 1698 and 1764, *etc.*

Kirk Bramwith

Kirk Bramwith, St. Mary, 1700-1970. Burial index **16**. Doncaster: Doncaster & District F.H.S., [1999?]. Not seen.

Kirk Deighton

MORTON, MAISIE, & PRESTON, CYRIL, eds. *The parish register of Kirk Deighton, 1600-1837.* Y.A.S., P.R.S. **159**. 1994. Includes terriers, list of clergy 1600-1837, list of churchwardens, 1722-1837, *etc.*

Kirk Ella

FOORD, JAMES, ed. *The register of Kirk Ella, Co. York: baptisms, 1558-1837; burials, 1558-1837; marriages, 1558-1841.* Parish Register Society, **11**. 1897.

Kirk Sandall

Kirk Sandall, 1679-1937. Burial index **3**. [Doncaster]: Doncaster & District F.H.S., 1998.

Kirk Smeaton

LAZENBY, BRENDA. *St. Peter, Kirk Smeaton: marriage index, 1813-1837.* Pontefract: Pontefract & District F.H.S., 1998.

Kirkburton

COLLINS, FRANCES ANNE, ed. *The parish registers of Kirkburton, Co.York.* 2 vols. Exeter: W. Pollard & Co., 1887-1902. v.1. 1541-1654. v.2. 1653-1711. Includes terriers, and extensive 'summaries of the history of Kirkburton families'.

WHITWAM, STEPHEN D. *Kirkburton parish church: baptisms 1711-1733.* Huddersfield: H. & D.F.H.S., 1990. Index only. Further volumes cover 1781-1789, 1789-1796, 1795-1812, 1813-1825, and 1825-1837.

ARMITAGE, JOHN S. 'Genealogical records of the parish of Kirkburton (part 1)', *H. & D.F.H.S.J.* 2(4), 1989, 92-3; 3(4), 1990, 94-8. Discussion of churches, their registers and burial grounds.

Kirkby Malham
OLIVER, W., ed. *The parish register of Kirkby Malham. Vol. 1. 1597-1690.* Y.P.R.S. 106. 1938. Also available on fiche. Includes list of vicars, 1585-1811.

Kirkheaton
Kirkheaton parish church baptisms, 1750-1772. Huddersfield: H. & D.F.H.S., 1994. Not seen.

Kirkleatham
CHARLESWORTH, JOHN, ed. *The parish register of Kirkleatham, Co. York, 1559-1812.* Y.P.R.S. 59. 1917. Also available on fiche.

Kirklington
MCCALL, H.B., ed. *The parish registers of Kirklington in the County of York, 1568-1812.* Y.P.R.S. 35. 1909.

Knaresborough
CUMMINS, THOMAS GEORGE, ENGELBACH, GEORGE FREDERICK, & HANSOM, JOSEPH STANISLAUS. 'The Catholic registers of Knaresborough, 1765-1840', in *Miscellanea* 12. C.R.S. 22. 1921, 220-75.
See also Harrogate

Knottingley
GOSNEY, RON. *St. Botolph parish church, Knottingley, in the West Riding of Yorkshire: baptism index, 1804-1812.* Pontefract: Pontefract & District F.H.S., 1998.
GOSNEY, RON. *St. Botolph, Knottingley, in the West Riding of Yorkshire: burial index, 1804-1812.* Pontefract: Pontefract & District F.H.S., 1998.
GOSNEY, RON. *St. Botolph parish church, Knottingley, in the West Riding of Yorkshire: marriage index 1813-1837.* Pontefract: Pontefract & District F.H.S., 1998.

GOSNEY, RON. *St. Botolph, Knottingley: baptism index, 1857-1886.* Pontefract & District F.H.S., 1998.
Baptisms solemnized in the Wesleyan Methodist Chapel, Knottingley, December 1838 - October 1922. Pontefract & District F.H.S., 1999. Not seen.

Laister Dyke
'[List of persons who died of Asiatic cholera in Bradford, 1849, buried at Greenhill Wesleyan Chapel, Laisterdyke]', *Bod-kin* 4, 1986, 8.

Laycock
Burial register for the Wesleyan Methodist Chapel at Laycock, near Keighley. Keighley: Keighley Family History Publishing, 1997. Index.

Ledsham
CLAY, J.W., ed. *The parish registers of Ledsham in the County of York, 1539-1812.* Y.P.R.S. 26. 1906. Also available on fiche.
LAZENBY, BRENDA. *All Saints parish church, Ledsham, in the West Riding of Yorkshire: marriage index 1813-1837.* Pontefract: Pontefract & District F.H.S., [1998?]

Leeds
M[ARGERISON], S., ed. *Leeds parish church registers: first and second books.* T.S. 1. 1891. 1572-1612.
LUMB, GEORGE DENISON, ed. *The registers of the parish church of Leeds, from 1612 to 1639: third and fourth books.* T.S. 3. 1895.
LUMB, GEORGE DENISON. *The registers of the parish church of Leeds from 1639 to 1667: fifth and sixth books.* T.S. 7. 1897.
LUMB, GEORGE DENISON, ed. *The registers of the parish church of Leeds from 1667 to 1695: seventh and eighth books.* T.S. 10. 1901.
LUMB, GEORGE DENISON, ed. *The registers of the parish church of Leeds from 1695 to 1722: ninth and tenth books, with Armley Chapel, 1665 to 1711, and Hunslet Chapel, 1686 to 1724.* T.S. 13. 1909.

LUMB, GEORGE DENISON, ed. *The registers of the parish church of Leeds from 1722 to 1757: eleventh and twelfth books.* T.S. **20**. 1914.

SINGLETON, JAMES, & HARGRAVE, EMILY, eds. *The registers of the parish church of Leeds: baptisms and burials, 1757 to 1776: thirteenth and fourteenth books. Marriages 1754 to 1769.* T.S. **25**. 1923. Supplemented by: 'Addenda to Leeds parish registers, 1757-1776: the parish registers of Saint Peter-at-Leeds', in *The Thoresby miscellany* **16**. T.S. **54**, 1979, 121. Baptisms April 26th-30th, 1775.

LUMB, GEORGE DENISON, ed. *The registers of the chapels of the parish church of Leeds from 1724 to 1763, with a few earlier years. St. John's, Holy Trinity, Armley, Beeston, Bramley, Chapel-Allerton, Farnley, Headingley, Holbeck and Hunslet. First and second books.* T.S. **23**. 1916.

LUMB, GEORGE DENISON, ed. *The registers of the chapels of St. John, Holy Trinity, Headingley, Bramley, Beeston, Chapel Allerton and Farnley, all in the parish of Leeds, from 1763 to 1812, and in some cases later years.* T.S. **29**. 1928.

LUMB, G.D. 'Burials at St. Paul's church, Leeds', in *Miscellanea* **[5]**. *T.S.* **15**, 1909, 56-70. For 1796-1865.

Strays and soldiers: from the marriage registers of the parish church of St. Peter at Leeds, 1769-1837. [Leeds]: [Y.A.S., F.H.P.S.S.], [199-].

'Strays: a collection of people who married outwith their normal place of residence or birth, taken from the marriage registers of the parish church of St. Peter, Leeds', *J.Cl.F.H.S.* **5**(5), 1993, 33-4. Late 18th-early 19th c.

See also Holbeck

Leyburn
See Danby

Linthwaite
WHITWAM, STEPHEN D. ed. *Linthwaite parish church: baptisms, marriages and burials, 1828-1860.* Huddersfield: H. & D.F.H.S., 1991.

Linton
SHARPE, F.A.C, ed. *The registers of the parish church of Linton in Craven, Co. York. Two volumes, 1562-1812. Vol. I (1562-1779).* Y.P.R.S. **5**. 1900. Also available on fiche.

SHARPE, F.A.C, ed. *The registers of the parish church of Linton in Craven, Co. York. Two volumes, 1562-1812. Vol. II (1779-1812).* Y.P.R.S. **18**. 1903. Also available on fiche.

Linton upon Ouse
HANSOM, JOSEPH STANISLAUS, ed. 'The Catholic registers of Linton-upon-Ouse, Newton-upon-Ouse, near York, 1771-1840', in *Miscellanea* **10**. C.R.S. **17**, 1915, 423-54.

Long Preston
HULL, NORAH,& HULL, ROLAND. *Long Preston Baptist church index of marriages contracted from March 1884 to March 1957.* L8. 1 fiche. [ ]: Lancashire Family History and Heraldry Society, Ribble Valley Branch, 1989.

HULL, NORAH, & HULL, ROLAND. *Long Preston Baptist church burial register: transcription 1836-1985.* **19**. 1 fiche. [ ]: Lancashire Family History and Heraldry Society, Ribble Valley Branch, 1989.

Lythe
HANSELL, M.W., ed. *The parish register of Lythe, volumes I, II & III, 1634-1768 (bishops transcripts, 1619-1640).* Y.A.S., P.R.S. **137**. 1973. Includes list of vicars, 1607-1858.

HANSELL, M.W., ed. *The parish register of Lythe, volumes IV-XI, 1754-1837.* Y.A.S., P.R.S. **138**. 1973.

Maltby
HUGHES, C.E., ed. *The register of the parish of Maltby, Co. York, 1597-1812.* Y.P.R.S. **81**. 1926.

Manfield
STAVERT, W.J., ed. *The parish register of Manfield in the County of York, 1594-1812.* Skipton: Craven Herald Office, 1898.

Marr
Marr, St. Helen, 1600-1973. Burial index **21**. Doncaster: Doncaster & District F.H.S., [1999?] Not seen.

Marsden
Marsden parish church baptisms, 1734-1782. Huddersfield: H. & D.F.H.S., 1994.

Marske
WOOD, HERBERT MAXWELL, ed. *The registers of Marske in Cleveland, Co. York. Baptisms 1570-1812; marriages 1570-1812; burials 1569-1812.* Y.P.R.S. **16**. 1903. Also available on fiche.

Masham
SMITH, DAVID M., ed. *The parish register of Masham, 1599-1716.* Y.A.S., P.R.S. **161**. 1996.

Methley
LUMB, GEORGE DENISON, ed. *The registers of the parish church of Methley in the County of York from 1560 to 1812.* T.S. **12**. 1903.
YASUMOTO, MINORU. 'How accurate is the Methley baptismal registration?', *Local population studies.* **35**, 1985, 19-24. Discussion of the parish registers, 18-19th c.

Mexborough
Cemetery burial registers: Mexborough ('new' burial ground) 1894-1938. 8 fiche. Doncaster: Doncaster & District F.H.S., [199-?]. Not seen.
Cemetery burial registers: Mexborough ('old' burial ground) 1878-1931. 12 fiche. Doncaster: Doncaster & District F.H.S., [199-?]. Not Seen.

Middlesbrough
BRADDY, JENNY. 'The register of buildings wherein marriages may be solemnised', *Cleveland history* **61**, 1991, 34-6. Discussion of 19th c. list held by the Middlesbrough Superintendant Registrar.

Middleton on the Wolds
Middleton-on-the-Wolds: parish registers 1678 to 1837. Cottingham: E.Y.F.H.S., 1984.

Middleton Tyas
SAYWELL, J.L. 'Middleton Tyas parochial history: extracts from banns book', *Y.C.M.* **4**, 1894, 247-52. 1832-64.

Mirfield
BRIGG, WILLIAM, ed. *The registers of the parish of Mirfield. Part I. Baptisms, marriages, burials, 1559-1700.* Y.P.R.S. **64**. 1919. Alternative title: *The parish registers of Mirfield, Co. York. Part I.* Also available on fiche.
LUMB, GEORGE DENISON, ed. *The register of the parish of Mirfield, Part II. Baptisms and burials, January 1700-March 1776. Marriages to March 1754.* Y.P.R.S., **72**. 1923.
WHITWAM, STEPHEN D., ed. *Mirfield parish church: baptisms 1813-1826.* Huddersfield: H. & D.F.H.S., 1991.

Monk Fryston
HEMSWORTH, J.D., ed. *The registers of Monk Fryston in the West Riding of Yorkshire, 1538-1678.* Parish Register Society, **5**. 1896.

Morley
See Topcliffe

Myton upon Swale
ROBINSON, HILARY I., ed. *The parish register of Myton upon Swale, 1654-1812.* Y.P.R.S. **121**. 1956.
See also Easingwold

Newton upon Ouse
See Linton upon Ouse

Nidd Hall
TRAPPES-LOMAX, RICHARD, ed. 'The Catholic registers of Nidd Hall, N.R. of York, 1780-1823', *Miscellanea* **3**. C.R.S., 3, 1906, 135-43. Actually in the West Riding.

Normanton
BRISCOE, GILL. *All Saints parish church, Normanton, in the West Riding of Yorkshire: marriage index 1813-1837.* Pontefract: Pontefract & District F.H.S., 1998.

Northowram
TURNER, J. HORSFALL, ed *The nonconformist register of baptisms, marriages and deaths, compiled by the Revs. Oliver Heywood & T. Dickenson, 1644-1702, 1702-1752, generally known as the Northowran or Coley register, but comprehending numerous notices of puritans and anti-puritans in Yorkshire, Lancashire, Cheshire, London, &c., with lists of popish recusants, Quakers, etc.* Brighouse: J.S. Jowett, 1881.

Norton le Clay
See Cundall

Nut Hill
BATERDEN, JAMES RAE, ed. 'The catholic register of Nut Hill and Hedon in Holderness, East Riding of Yorkshire', in *Miscellanea*. C.R.S., **35**. 1936. 1774-1849.

Ossett
JONES, BRIAN. *Ossett Wesley Street Wesleyan Chapel: baptisms, 1795-1845.* Bradford: Brian Jones, 1998.

Oswaldkirk
ROWLEY, PATRICK, ed. *The parish register of Oswaldkirk, vols. I-X, 1538-1837.* Y.P.R.S. **135**. 1976. Includes 'notes on Oswaldkirk clergy, during the period covered by this volume'.

Otley
BRIGG, WILLIAM, ed. *The parish registers of Otley, Co. York. Part 1. 1562 to 1672.* Y.P.R.S. **33**. 1908. Also available on fiche.
BRIGG, WILLIAM, ed. *The parish registers of Otley, Co. York. Part 2. Bap., April 1672 to June 1753; Marr., April 1672 to June 1750; Bur., April 1672 to March 1751-2.* Y.P.R.S. **44**. 1912. Also available on fiche.
'Otley parish registers', *Y.N.Q.I.* **2**, 1890, 253-4. Brief discussion with a few extracts.

Owston
BRENT, ANDREW, ed. *The parish register of Owston, 1600-1837.* Y.A.S., P.R.S. **157**. 1993. Includes list of clergy 1598-1845, and churchwardens, 1600-1837.

Paddock
WHITWAM, STEPHEN D., ed. *Paddock parish church: baptisms, marriages and burials, 1830-1870.* Huddersfield: H. & D.F.H.S., 1994.

Patrington
MADDOCK, HENRY EDWARD, ed. *The registers of Patrington, Co. York, 1570-1731.* Y.P.R.S. **6**. 1900. Also available on fiche.

Pickering
See Pocklington

Pickhill
HOWARD, ARTHUR W., ed. *The registers of Pickhill cum Roxby, Co. York. Marriages 1567-1812; baptisms 1571-1812; burials 1576-1812.* Y.P.R.S. **20**. 1904.

Pocklington
ROBSON, JAMES. 'Pocklington church, Yorkshire', *Northern notes and queries* **1**, 1906, 227-30. Includes a few parish register extracts, etc.
WHYTEHEAD, T.B. 'Marriage bonds of the peculiar jurisdiction of the Deanery of York', *Northern genealogist* **6**, 1903, 69-73. For 1764-9; Pocklington and Pickering area.

Pontefract
WILLIS, THOMAS B., ed. *The parish register of Pontefract, 1585-1641.* Y.P.R.S. **122**. 1958. Also available on fiche.
GOSNEY, RON. *St. Giles parish church, Pontefract, in the West Riding of Yorkshire: burial index, 1751-1776.* Pontefract: Pontefract & District F.H.S., 1999. Further volumes by various editors cover 1777-1790, 1791-1800, 1801-1812, 1813-1820, and 1821-1834.
GOSNEY, RON, LAZENBY, BRENDA, & BRISCOE, GILL. *St. Giles parish church, Pontefract, in the West Riding of Yorkshire: marriage index, 1813-1837.* 2 vols. Pontefract & District F.H.S., 1998.
ALLEN, D. 'Some extracts from the parochial magazine, All Saints church, Pontefract, 1877', *Y.A.S., F.H.P.S.S.N.* **5**, 1975, 66-8. Baptisms, marriages and burials.
Baptisms solemnized in the Wesleyan Methodist chapel, Pontefract, 1838-1874. Pontefract: Pontefract & District F.H.S., 1999. Not seen.

Raskelf
ROBINSON, HILARY I., ed. *The parish registers of Raskelf, 1747-1812.* Y.P.R.S. **119**. 1953. *See also* Easingwold

Rawcliffe
Rawcliffe St. James, 1753-1900. Burial index 8-9. 2 vols. Doncaster: Doncaster & District F.H.S., 1998.

Rawdon

WOLSTENHULME, LES, & CLAYTON, BRIAN, eds. *Friend's burial ground, Quaker's Lane, Rawdon. Alphabetical list of burials 1695-1976, & memorial inscriptions in the burial ground 1830-1993.* Burley in Wharfedale: Wharfedale Family History Group, 1997.

WOLSTENHULME, LES, & CLAYTON, BRIAN, eds. *Greenhill Wesleyan Methodist Church, Rawdon: burials 1905-1961, & memorial inscriptions 1836-1961.* Burley in Wharfedale: Wharfedale Family History Group, 1997.

Riccall

HAMSHAW, ROBERT GORDON, ed. *The parish register of Riccall, Yorks., 1669-1813 [marriages end 1753].* Y.P.R.S. **124.** 1960.

Richmond Archdeaconry

See Richmondshire

Richmondshire

WAINE, W.G., ed. *The register of the civil marriages, 1653- 1660, belonging to Richmondshire in the County of York.* Y.P.R.S. **101.** 1936. Also includes OLIVER, W., ed. *Index to the parish register transcripts belonging to the Archdeaconry of Richmond (the ancient deaneries of Boroughbridge, Catterick and Richmond) from their commencement to 1848.* Y.P.R.S. 1936. Also available on fiche.

Rillington

WHITING, C.E., ed. *The parish registers of Rillington, 1638-1812.* Y.P.R.S. **117.** 1946. Also available on fiche.

Ripon

KAYE, W.J., ed. *The parish register of Ripon. Part I. (1574-1628).* Y.P.R.S. **80.** 1926.
Ripon parish registers; C. 1572-1855, B. 1574-1881; M. 1576-June 1837; index to marriage witnesses. 6 fiche. Ripon & Harrogate F.H.S., 1997.
HEBDEN, JOHN. 'Parish registers of the Ripon area', *R.H.* 1(2), 1989, 7-8. Brief discussion.

Rokeby

ALDERSON, BASIL ROXBY, ed. *The parish register of Rokeby, Yorks.,* vols I-VII, 1598-1837. Y.P.R.S. **128.** 1965.

Romaldkirk

BELL, G. *Romaldkirk baptisms, marriages and burials, 1813-1839.* 2 fiche. Wideopen: Original index, 1997. Index only.

Roos

MACHELL, RICHARD BEVERLEY, ed. *Register for the parish of All Saints, Roos, Holderness, East-Riding of Yorkshire.* Hull: A. Brown & Sons, 1888. Vol. 1. 1571-1678. No more published.

Rotherham

GUEST, JOHN, ed. *County of York: early parish register of Rotherham.* Workshop: Robert White, 1879. Reprinted from his *Historic notices of Rotherham.*
JAMES, C.S., ed. *Yorkshire marriage registers, West Riding. Vol. 1.* Phillimores Parish Register Series **201.** 1914. This volume contains the Rotherham marriage register 1540-1798 only.
GOODALL, J.W., ed. *Rotherham, part II. (1798-1837 and index.)* Yorkshire Marriage Registers West Riding. 2. Phillimores Parish Register Series **217.** 1915.

Rothwell

LUMB, GEORGE DENISON, ed. *The registers of the parish church of Rothwell, Co. York. Part I. 1538-1689.* Y.P.R.S. **27.** 1906. Also available on fiche.
LUMB, GEORGE DENISON, ed. *The registers of the parish church of Rothwell, Co. York. Part II. 1690-1763, baptisms and burials; 1690-1812 marriages.* Y.P.R.S. **34.** 1909. Also available on fiche.
LUMB, GEORGE DENISON, ed. *The registers of the parish church of Rothwell, Co. York. Part III. 1763-1812. Baptisms and burials. Index.* Y.P.R.S. **51.** 1914. Also available on fiche.

Routh

PATTINSON, P.M., ed. *Routh: marriages 1750-1837.* East Riding transcripts **1.** Willerby: E.Y.F.H.S., [198-].

Roxby
See Pickhill

Rudby in Cleveland
See East Rounton

Rylstone
LOWE, C.H., ed. *The register of St. Peter's, Rylstone (formerly part of the ancient parish of Burnsall).* 2 vols. Leeds: Petty & Sons, 1895-6. v. 1. 1559-1723. v.2. 1724-1812.

Saddleworth
RADCLIFFE, JOHN, ed. *The parish registers of St. Chad, Saddleworth, in the County of York, containing the marriages, baptisms and burials from 1613 to 1751 ...* Uppermill: the editor, 1887. Includes extensive extracts from other miscellaneous sources, and descent of the manor of Saddleworth.
RADCLIFFE, JOHN. *The parish registers of St. Chad, Saddleworth, in the County of York, containing the marriages, baptisms and burials from 1751 to 1800, with baptisms and burials from the chapels of Heights, Dobcross, and Lydgate, also supplement and appendix containing information respecting the church and parish of Saddleworth-cum-Quick.* Uppermill: John Moore, 1891. Includes banns, 1754-88, biographical notes on clergy, clerks and sextons, list of churchwardens, monumental inscriptions, extracts from parish records, *etc., etc.*
Marriage index, 1800-1837 for St. Chad's parish church of Saddleworth, Greater Manchester County, (formerly West Riding of Yorkshire). S7. 2 fiche. [ ]: [Rossendale Society for Genealogy and Herladry], 1985.
'Saddleworth entries in the Ashton church registers', *B.S.H.S.* 10(1), 1980, 5-7. 1598-1710. (i.e. Ashton under Lyne, Lancashire).

Salendine Nook
Salendine Nook Baptist Church: dedications 1783 to 1822. Huddersfield: H. & D.F.H.S., 1993. Not seen.

Sandal Magna
'Sandal Magna parish register', *Northern genealogist* **3**, 1900, 160-8; **4**, 1901, 52-6 & 81-4. Bishops' transcripts, 1598-1631 (not all).

Saxton in Elmet
LUMB, GEORGE DENISON, ed. *The parish register of Saxton-in-Elmet, 1538-1812.* Y.P.R.S. **93**. 1932. Also available on fiche.

Scampston
See Rillington

Scarborough
'Quaker extracts from some Yorkshire parish registers', *Friends Historical Society journal* **32**, 1936, 50. From Scarborough, Grinton, *etc.*

Scorborough
See Blacktoft

Scruton
PRESTON, C.S., ed. *The parish register of Scruton, 1572-1837.* Y.A.S., P.R.S. **156**. 1991. Includes lists of clergy and churchwardens, 'stray' marriages, *etc.*

Sculcoates
INGRAM, M. EDWARD, ed. *The parish register of Sculcoates (part 1) 1538-1772.* Y.P.R.S. **123**. 1959. Also available on fiche.
Sculcoates: baptisms, 1772-1789; burials, 1772-1792. Cottingham. E.Y.F.H.S., 1993.
Baptisms solemnized in the parish of Sculcoates in the County of York, September 1806 to December 1812. Cottingham: E.Y.F.H.S., 1997.
Sculcoates baptisms January 1813 to December 1820. [ ]: E.Y.F.H.S., [1989?] Further volumes cover January 1821 to June 1831, and July 1831 to December 1837.
Sculcoates: marriages, January 1813 to April 1821. Cottingham: E.Y.F.H.S., [1993]. Further volumes cover April 1821 to December 1829 (1995), and January 1830 to June 1837 (1995).
Burials in the parish of Sculcoates in the County of York, January 1813 to September 1824. Cottingham: E.Y.F.H.S., 1991. A further volume covers September 1824 to December 1831. (1992).

Seamer
GADD, BILL, ed. *Seamer parish registers 1813-1837.* East Riding transcripts **4**. Cottingham: E.Y.F.H.S., 1991.

Sedburgh

WINN, ARTHUR T., ed. *The registers of the parish church of Sedbergh, Co. York, 1594-1800.* 3 vols. Sedbergh: Jackson & Son, 1912. v.1. Baptisms. v. 2. Marriages. v.3. Burials.

Selby

'A record of all the marriages, births and burials of the people of God (called by the world Quakers) belonging to the Selby meeting', *C.Y.D.F.H.S.* **31**, 1993, 8. For 1651-69.

Sessay

FISHER, T.M., ed. *The parish register of Sessay, near Thirsk. Contents: baptisms 1600-1812; marriages 1600-1812; burials 1600- 1812; list of rectors 1624-1937; briefs 1662-1690.* Y.P.R.S. **103**. 1937.

Settrington

COLLINS, FRANCIS, ed. *The register of Settrington, 1559-1812.* Y.P.R.S. **38**. 1910.

Sheffield

DRURY, CHARLES, & HALL, T. WALTER, eds. *The parish register of Sheffield in the County of York. Part I. Baptisms and marriages, 1560 to 1634-5.* Sheffield: Hunter Archaeaolgical Society, 1917. Jointly published as Y.P.R.S. **58**.

DRURY, CHARLES, & HALL, T. WALTER, eds. *The parish register of Sheffield in the County of York. Part II. Burials 1560 to 1634; baptisms, marriages 1635 to 1653.* Y.P.R.S. **60**. 1918.

DRURY, CHARLES, & HALL, T. WALTER, eds. *The parish register of Sheffield in the County of York. Part III. Burials, 1635 to 1653; baptisms, marriages, 1653 to 1686.* Y.P.R.S. **68**. 1921.

DRURY, CHARLES, & HALL, T. WALTER, eds. *The parish register of Sheffield in the County of York, part IV: burials 1653 to 1686; baptisms 1687 to 1703; marriages 1687 to 1703.* Sheffield: Hunter Archaeological Society, 1924. Also published as Y.P.R.S. **74**. 1924.

HALL, T. WALTER, ed. *The parish register of Sheffield in the County of York. Part V. Burials, 1686 to 1703. Baptisms 1703 to 1719. Marriages, 1703 to 1719.* Sheffield: Hunter Archaeological Society, 1927.

OWEN, W.S., & WALTON, MARY, eds. *The parish register of Sheffield, volume VI. 1720-1736.* Y.A.S., P.R.S. **143**. 1981.

WALTON, MARY, & OWEN, W.S., eds. *The parish register of Sheffield. Volume 7. Burials 1703-1719; baptisms 1736-1752.* Y.A.S., P.R.S. **154**. 1989.

WIGFULL, JAMES R. 'The early books of the parish register of Sheffield', *T.Hunter A.S.* **2**(1), 1920 82-108. General discussion.

'Copy of a register of children baptised by the Rev. Mr [Timothy] Jollie, [Sheffield] from April 18, 1681 [the day of his ordination] to July 27 1704', *Y.N.Q.I.* **2**, 1890, 40-48.

'Burial grounds in and around Sheffield', *F.S.* **13**(2), 1992, 34-9. List with details of registers and transcripts of inscriptions available.

Silkstone

SQUIRE, J.T. 'Notes from Silkstone registers', *Y.N.Q.I.* **1**, 1888, 236-8. Extracts, 1655-1715.

Silsden

'Non-conformists baptisms at Silsden', *K.D.F.H.S.J.* Winter 1994, 8-9. Late 19th c., various chapels.

Skelbrooke

BRENT, ANDREW, ed. *The parish register of Skelbrooke in the County of York (W.R.) 1592-1836.* Doncaster: Doncaster and District F.H.S., 1993.

See also South Kirby

Skelton

'List of people from outside Skelton who married there, 1722- 1750', *J.Cl.F.H.S.* **2**(5), 1983, 14-15.

Skipsea

PATTINSON, P.M., ed. *Skipsea marriages, 1750-1837.* East Riding transcripts **3**. Cottingham: E.Y.F.H.S., [198-].

Skipton

STAVERT, W.J., ed. *The parish register of Skipton-in-Craven, 1592-1680.* Skipton: Craven Herald Office, 1894.

STAVERT, W.J., ed. *The parish register of Skipton-in-Craven, 1680-1771.* Skipton: Craven Herald Office, 1895.

STAVERT, W.J., ed. *The parish register of Skipton-in-Craven, 1745-1812.* Skipton: Craven Herald Office, 1896.

PRESTON, R. 'Gems from a parish register', *Family tree magazine* 4(9), 1988, 7. Extracts from Skipton, Yorkshire, parish register.

Slaidburn

SPENCER, C.J.,& POSTLETHWAITE, R.H., eds. *The registers of the parish church of St. Andrew, Slaidburn, Lancashire (Yorkshire pre-1974) 1600-1770.* [ ]: privately published, 1994. A further volume, published 1998, covers baptisms and marriages, 1771-1837, and burials, 1771-1852.

Slaithwaite

Slaithwaite parish church baptisms, 1685-1726. Huddersfield: H. & D.F.H.S., 1995. Not seen.

Slaithwaite parish church baptisms, 1727-1760. Huddersfield: H. & D.F.H.S., 1995. Not seen.

Snaith

BRIGG, WILLIAM, ed. *The parish registers of Snaith, Co. York. Part I. Baptisms 1558-1657. Marriages 1537-1657.* Y.P.R.S. 57. 1917. Also available on fiche.

BRIGG, WILLIAM, ed. *The parish registers of Snaith, Co. York. Part II. Burials 1537-1656.* Y.P.R.S. 63. 1919. Also available on fiche.

BRIGG, WILLIAM. 'Snaith marriage licences', *Y.A.J.* 20, 1908-9, 225-32. For 1596-1628 and 1715-54.

South Cave

RICHARDSON, WILLIAM. *The parish registers of South Cave, East Yorkshire with notes thereon.* Hull: A. Brown & Sons, 1909. Includes notes on a few wills, census return 1831, appendices on the families of Cave and Ellerker, *etc.*

South Crosland

South Crosland parish church baptisms, marriages and burials 1829-1855. Huddersfield: H. & D.F.H.S., 1994. Not seen.

South Holderness

MADDOCK, H.E. 'Parish registers of South Holderness', *T.E.R.A.S.* 5, 1897, 1-34. Reprinted as *Malet Lambert local history reprints* 29. Hull: A.G. Bell, [198-?] Discussion, with brief extracts.

South Kirby

BRISCOE, GILL, & BUCHANAN, SHARON. *All Saints parish church, South Kirby, in the West Riding of Yorkshire: marriage index, 1813-1837.* Pontefract: Pontefract & District F.H.S., 1998. Cover title: *All Saints, South Kirby & Skelbrooke marriage index 1813-1837.*

Sprotborough

Sprotborough, St. Mary the Virgin, 1559-1910. Burial index 17-18. 2 vols. Doncaster: Doncaster & District F.H.S., [1999?] Not seen.

Startforth

BULLEN, MARK W. 'Startforth parish register, Co. York', *Northern genealogist* 2, 1896, 89-96 & 143-52; 3, 1900, 54-6, 105-8 & 150-53. 1665-1700.

Stokesley

HAWELL, JOHN, ed. *The registers of the parish church of Stokesley, Co. York, 1571-1750.* Y.P.R.S. 7. 1900. Also available on fiche.

Swillington

GEORGE, E., ed. *The parish register of Swillington, Yorks. Baptisms 1543-1812. Marriages 1540-1812. Burials 1539-1812.* Y.P.R.S. 115. 1944. Also available on fiche.

Swinefleet

Swinefleet, St. Margaret. 2 vols. Burial index 14-15. Doncaster: Doncaster & District F.H.S., [1998?] Not seen.

Terrington

BRIGG, WILLIAM, ed. *The registers of Terrington, Co. York. Christenings, 1600-1812; marriages, burials, 1599-1812.* Y.P.R.S. 29. 1907.

Thirsk

PARKER, JOHN, ed. *The parish register of Thirsk in the County of York, North Riding, 1556-1721.* Y.P.R.S. **42**. 1911.

Thorne

'Register of marriages at Thorne, near Doncaster', *Family history* **5**(32/33); N.S., **8/9**, 1970, 236-61; **7**(38/39); N.S., **14/15**, 1972, 60-64 & 72. 1556-1697.

Thornhill

CHARLESWORTH, JOHN, ed. *The register of the parish of Thornhill, part I. Baptisms 1580 to 1742; marriages 1580 to 1745; burials 1580 to 1678.* Y.P.R.S. **30**. 1907. Also available on fiche.

CHARLESWORTH, JOHN, ed. *The register of the parish of Thornhill, part II. Baptisms 1743 to 1812; marriages 1746 to 1753; burials 1678 to 1812; Flockton baptisms, marriages and burials, 1713 to 1812.* Y.P.R.S.**40**. 1911. Also available on fiche.

CHARLESWORTH, JOHN, ed. *The register of the parish of Thornhill, part III. Marriages 1754 to 1812; banns 1788 to 1812; Flockton baptisms and burials 1717 to 1812.* Y.P.R.S. **53**. 1915. Also available on fiche.

Thornton

JONES, BRIAN, & LUMB, E. MAUD. *Thornton Wesleyan Methodist Chapel: baptisms 1817 to 1837, and 'Methodism in Thornton: the reminiscences of John Craven'.* Bradford: Brian Jones, 1997.

Thornton Bell Chapel. 6 fiche. Bradford: Bradford F.H.S., 1996. Index to marriages 1732-51 and baptisms 1731-85; burials 1731-87.

See also Kipping

Thornton in Lonsdale

CHIPPINDALL, W.H., ed. *The parish register of Thornton-in-Lonsdale (1576-1812).* Y.P.R.S. **89**. 1931. Also available on fiche.

Thorpe Bassett

RUDDOCK, N.P., ed. *The parish register of Thorpe Bassett, 1604-1837.* Y.P.R.S. **155**. 1990.

Thorpe Salvin

BROWNE, G. OSBOURNE. 'Registers of Thorpe-Salvin, Co. York', *Y.C.M.* **2**, 1892, 49-80 & 129-50. 1592-1726.

BROWNE, G. OSBOURNE. *Registers of Thorpe-Salvin, Co. York.* Bingley: Harrison & Sons, 1892. Reprinted from the *Yorkshire County Magazine.* Covers 1592-1726.

Thruscross

COE, SHEILA. 'Records of Thruscross Chapel', *Wh. N.* **24**, 1997, 18-20. Discussion of register entries, with some extracts 1719-22, *etc.*

Tong

JONES, BRIAN. *Saint James church, Tong, in the parish of Birstall: marriages 1728 to 1753.* Bradford: Brian Jones, 1997. Further volumes cover 1754 to 1781 (1996), 1782 to 1801 (1996), and 1802 to 1814 (1997).

Topcliffe

SMITH, WILLIAM, ed. *The registers of Topcliffe and Morley, in the W.R. of the County of York. Baptisms 1654-1830, Burials 1654-1888.* Longmans Green and Co., 1888. Includes list of Morley ministers and monumental inscriptions.

Waddington

PARKER, JOHN, ed. *The parish registers of Waddington, Yorkshire (1599-1812).* Y.P.R.S. **88**. 1930. Also available on fiche.

Wadworth

PRESTON, CYRIL, ed. *The parish register of Wadworth, 1575- 1837.* Y.A.S., P.R.S. **162**. 1997.

SYKES, JOHN. 'Extracts from the parish register of Wadworth', *Y.A.J.* **9**, 1886, 470-76.

Walton

FLETCHER, D.E., & FLETCHER, C.E., eds. *The parish register of Walton in Ainsty, vols I-IV. 1619-1837.* Y.P.R.S. **126**. 1962.

Warmsworth

Warmsworth, St. Peter, 1596-1716. Burial index **19**. Doncaster: Doncaster & District F.H.S., [1999?]. Not seen.

Wath juxta Ripon

W., J. 'Extracts from the parish registers of Wath, near Ripon', *Topographer & genealogist* **3**, 1858, 414-36. See also 591-6.

Wath upon Dearne

CLAY, J.W., ed. *The registers of Wath-upon-Dearne, Yorkshire. Baptisms and burials, 1598-1778; marriages, 1598-1779.* Y.P.R.S. **14**. 1902. Also available on fiche.

Welwick

PATTINSON, P.M., ed. *Welwick marriages, 1754-1837.* East Riding transcripts **4**. Willerby: E.Y.F.H.S., 1985.

Wensley

OLIVER, W., ed. *The parish register of Wensley, in the County of York. Vol. I. 1538-1700.* Y.P.R.S. **108**. 1939.

THWAITE, HARTLEY, ed. *The parish register of Wensley. Vol. II. 1701-1837.* Y.P.R.S. **130**. 1967. Includes 'notes on Wensley clergy'.

'Notes from Wensley register', *Y.N.Q.II.* **1**, 1905, 317-8. Extracts only, 16-18th c.

West Witton

See Danby

Westerdale

FEATHERSTONE, STANLEY SWITHIN. 'Village undertakers', *J.Cl.F.H.S.* **4**(6), 1990, 48-9. List of persons for whom Thomas Featherstone of Westerdale made coffins, 1893-1936.

Whitby

CHARLESWORTH, JOHN, ed. *The parish register of Whitby, 1600- 1676. Part I.* Y.P.R.S. **84**. 1928. Also available on fiche.

Whitkirk

PLATT, GEORGE MORETON, & MORKILL, JOHN WILLIAM. *Records of the parish of Whitkirk.* Leeds: Richard Jackson, 1892. Includes full transcript of the parish register, 1603-1700, extracts from churchwardens accounts, 1653/4-1687/8, manorial descents, pedigrees, *etc.*

'Whitkirk register: transcripts at York', in *Miscellanea* **[6]**. *T.S.* **22**, 1915, 103-6. 1600-1601.

Winestead

MILLER, NORMAN J., ed. *The registers of Winestead in Holderness, Co. York, 1578-1812.* Y.P.R.S. **4**. 1899. Also available on fiche.

Wintringham

CHOLMLEY, ALFRED J., ed. *The parish register of Wintringham (1558 to 1812).* Y.P.R.S. **71**. 1922. Also available on fiche.

Womersley

LAZENBY, BRENDA. *St. Martin, Womersley: marriage index, 1754-1812.* Pontefract: Pontefract & District F.H.S., 1998.

LAZENBY, BRENDA. *St. Martin, Womersley: marriage index, 1813-1837.* Pontefract: Pontefract & District F.H.S., 1998.

Worsbrough

ASHURST, DENNIS. 'St Marys church, Worsbrough, Yorkshire: a review of the accuracy of a parish register', *Local population studies* **55**, 1995, 46-57. See also 58-60.

Wragby

CHARLESWORTH, JOHN, ed. *The parish register of Wragby vol. I. 1538-1704, containing baptisms, marriages and burials, 1538-1552, 1557-1567, 1570-1704; churchwardens' accounts, 1604-1612, 1618-1620, 1625; overseers of the highways accounts, 1626-1627, 1630-1631; will of Robert Holgate, Archbishop of York, dated 27 April 1555, and rental of estate, 1572; briefs 1661-1664, 1667, 1671-1672, 1674-1675, 1682.* Y.P.R.S. **105**. 1938. Also available on fiche.

CHARLESWORTH, JOHN, ed. *The parish register of Wragby in the County of York. Vol. II. 1704-1812.* Y.P.R.S.**107**. 1939. Also available on fiche.

BRISCOE, GILL. *St. Michael parish church, Wragby, in the West Riding of Yorkshire: marriage index 1813-1837.* Pontefract: Pontefract & District F.H.S., [1998?]

SANKEY, E.H. 'Wragby registers, book no. 1', *Y.A.J.* **12**, 1893, 309-16. General discussion of the parish register, but few extracts.

SANKEY, EDWARD H. 'Wragby registers, book no. II', *Y.A.J.* **13**, 1895, 213-8. General discussion, includes some extracts.
SANKEY, EDWARD H. 'Wragby registers, book no. III', *Y.A.J.* **14**, 1896-7, 313-26. General discussion; includes extracts.

Yeadon

WOLSTENHULME, LES, & CLAYTON, BRIAN. *Primitive Methodist Chapel, Town Hall Square, Yeadon: burials (1844) & 1852-1944, & memorial inscriptions.* Leeds: Wharfedale Family History Group, 1897. Burial register with inscriptions.

York

York marriage index, 1701-1750. 4 fiche. York: City of York & District F.H.S., 1990.
York marriage index, 1751-1800. 4 fiche. York: York F.H.S., 1987.
York marriage index, 1801-1837. 4 fiche. York: York F.H.S., 1987.

All Saints, Pavement

FISHER, T.M., ed. *The parish register of All Saints church, Pavement, in the City of York. Vol. I. 1554-1690, containing baptisms, 1554-1690, marriages 1555-1690, burials 1554-1689, burials in the church, 1643-1690.* Y.P.R.S. **100**. 1935.
FISHER, T.M., ed. *The parish register of All Saints Church, Pavement, in the City of York. Vol. II, containing baptisms 1690-1738, marriages, 1690-1738, burials 1690-1792, with indexes to vols. I. and II.* Y.P.R.S. **102**. 1936.
'The parish register of All Saints, Pavement, York: marriages 1555-1690', *Northern genealogist* **6**, 1903, 64-8. For 1555-1611.

Holy Trinity, Goodramgate

COOK, ROBERT BEILBY, ed. *The parish registers of Holy Trinity church, Goodramgate, York, 1573-1812.* Y.P.R.S. **41**. 1911. Also available on fiche. Includes list of rectors, 13-20th c., and list of testators requesting burial in the church, 1386-1566.
HUNT, SUSAN, ed. *The parish registers of Holy Trinity, Goodramgate, York, 1813-1837.* York F.H.S. publications **4**. 1980.

'Naval and military notes: parish registers of Holy Trinity, Goodramgate, York', *Northern genealogist* **2**, 1896, 49-52 & 111-3. Extracts of baptisms and burials, 1640-1799; also includes a few wills.

Holy Trinity, Kings Court

KAYE, WALTER J., ed. *The parish register of Holy Trinity, Kings Court (otherwise Christ Church), York (1716-1812, with additions from 1631).* Y.P.R.S. **85**. 1928.
YORK FAMILY HISTORY SOCIETY, ed. *The parish registers of Holy Trinity, King's Court, York, 1813-1837.* York F.H.S. publications **2**. 1979.

Holy Trinity, Micklegate

BATEMAN, W.H.F., ed. *The parish registers of Holy Trinity, Micklegate, in the City of York.* 4 pts. York: Delittle & Sons, [1893]-5. Covers 1585-1777.

St. Crux

COOK, R. BEILBY, & HARRISON, F., eds. *The parish register of St Crux, York. Part I. (1539-1716).* Y.P.R.S. **70**. 1922.
SMITH, MARGARET E., ed. *The parish register of St. Crux, York. Volume II. Baptisms 1716-1837; marriages and burials 1678-1837.* Y.A.S., P.R.S. **149**. 1985.

St. Laurence

HUDSON, EGBERT CLAUD, ed. *The parish register of St. Laurence, York (1606-1812).* Y.P.R.S. **97**. 1935. Also available on fiche. Includes lists of clergy.

St. Martin, Coney Street

COOK, ROBERT BEILBY, ed. *The parish registers of St. Martin, Coney Street, York.* Y.P.R.S. **36**. 1909. Also available on fiche. For 1557-1812.
SMITH, MARGARET E., ed. *The parish registers of St. Martin, Coney Street, York, 1813-1837.* York F.H.S. publications **1**. 1978.

St Martin cum Gregory

BULMER, EDWARD, ed. *The parish registers of St Martin-cum-Gregory in the City of York ... vols I and II from A.D. 1539-1734, and index.* York: Delittle & Sons, 1897.

St. Mary Bishophill Junior

COLLINS, FRANCIS, ed. *The parish register of St. Mary, Bishophill Junior 1602 to 1812.* Y.P.R.S. **52**. 1915.

YORK FAMILY HISTORY SOCIETY, ed. *The parish registers of St. Mary, Bishophill Junior, York, 1813-1837.* York F.H.S. publications **5**. 1981.

St. Mary, Castlegate

MULGREW, M. LOYOLA, ed. *The parish register of St. Mary, Castlegate, York. Volume I. 1604-1705.* Y.P.R.S. **134**. 1970. Includes list of rectors, 1233-1837.

MULGREW, MARGARET F.M., ed. *The parish register of St. Mary, Castlegate, York. Volumes II, III & IV, 1705-1837 (bishops' transcripts, 1813-1837).* Y.A.S., P.R.S. **136**. 1972.

SKAIFE, ROBERT H. 'Extracts from the registers of the church of St. Mary, Castlegate, York, with biographical and other notes', *Y.A.J.* **15**, 1898-9, 142-98. Baptisms, 1612-1859; marriages, 1615-1792; burials, 1604-1844. Also includes 'testamentary burials', i.e. extracts from wills, 14-16th c., of persons desiring burial in the church.

St. Maurice

'Marriage registers of St. Maurice, York (a complete abstract)', *Northern genealogist* **3**, 1900, 181-4; **4**, 1901, 39-41 & 88-92; **5**, 1902, 96-8. For 1648-1812.

St. Michael le Belfrey

COLLINS, FRANCIS, ed. *The registers of St. Michael le Belfrey, York. Part I. 1565-1653.* Y.P.R.S. **1**. 1899. Also available on fiche.

COLLINS, FRANCIS, ed. *The register of St. Michael le Belfrey, York. Part II. Marriages 1653-1772; baptisms and burials 1653-1778.* Y.P.R.S. **11**. 1901. Also available on fiche.

St. Olave

HARRISON, F., & KAYE, WALTER J., eds. *The parish register of St. Olave, York. Part I (1538-1644).* Y.P.R.S. **73**. 1923. Also available on fiche.

WHITEHEAD, BARBARA, ed. *The parish register of St. Olave, York, 1650-1785.* Y.A.S., P.R.S. **158**. 1993.

'Strays on the burial index', *C.Y.D.F.H.S.J.* **45**, 1998, 24-7. Includes list of burials at St. Olaves, York, of York Asylum patients.

York Castle

BAXTER, JEANNE. 'York Castle', *Y.F.H.S.N.* **6**, 1982, 11-12. Register of prisoners' deaths, 1731-43, and of baptisms for the same period, from Y.A.S. mss.489.

MORTON, MAISIE. 'An archive treasure', *Y.F.H.* **17**(6), 1991, 157-60. Burials at York Castle, 1730-43, plus a few baptisms.

'Register of York Castle, 1730-1743', *Y.A.J.* **25**, 1920, 437-41. Burials, including executions.

York Minster

SKAIFE, ROBERT H. 'The register of baptisms in York Minster', *Y.A.J.* **6**, 1881, 385-95. 1686-1804.

SKAIFE, ROBERT H. 'The register of marriages in York Minster', *Y.A.J.* **2**, 1837, 97-128 & 321-70; **3**, 1875, 81-146. 1681-1762.

SKAIFE, ROBERT H. 'The register of burials in York Minster, accompanied by monumental inscriptions, and illustrated with biographical notices', *Y.A.J.* **1**, 1870, 226-330. For 1634-1836.

Baptist

BERRYMAN, P. 'Early York baptists', *C.Y.D.F.H.S.J.* **27**, 1992, 28-30. Discussion of the register of York Baptist Church; many names, 18-19th c.

Roman Catholics

HANSOM, JOSEPH S., et al, eds. 'The Catholic registers of Little Blake Street Chapel, now St. Wilfred's York, 1771-1838', in *Miscellanea.* C.R.S. **35**, 1936, 1-197.

HANSOM, JOSEPH S. 'The catholic registers of York Bar convent chapel, being the conventual chapel of the Institute of Mary, outside Micklegate Bar 1771-1826', in *Miscellanea* 4. C.R.S. **4**, 1907, 374-410.

Society of Friends

'Notes on the Quakers' registers at York', *Northern genealogist* **1**, 1895, 245.

2. MONUMENTAL INSCRIPTIONS etc.

A. General

Monumental inscriptions are a vital source of genealogical information, and many are available in print or on fiche. Numerous inscriptions contained in works of wider interest are mentioned in other parts of this bibliography. Family history societies have been particularly active in the last two decades recording inscriptions in graveyards throughout Yorkshire. Much of this work has been published, and is listed in section B below. The locations of recorded inscriptions, both published and unpublished, are listed in:

Where to find recorded monumental inscriptions, Yorkshire. New ed. [ ]: North East Group of Family History Societies, 1998.

A now rather out of date listing of monumental inscriptions at Sheffield is provided in:

SHEFFIELD RECORD OFFICE. *Family history guide no. 2. Monumental inscriptions.* Sheffield: Sheffield City Libraries, [198-?]
For a very out of date listing, which may still be worth consulting, see:
'Yorkshire monumental inscriptions: a list of 84 transcripts printed and in ms', *Register of English monumental inscriptions* 2, 1914, 89-93.
Some of the works listed in volume 1, section 3 of this bibliography provide listings of inscriptions in other parts of the county. There are very few general publications on Yorkshire monumental inscriptions; most that are available deal with brasses, effigies and heraldry. See, however:
DODSWORTH, ROGER. *Yorkshire church notes, 1619-1631,* ed. J.W.Clay. Y.A.S., R.S. 34. 1904. Notes made on visits to Yorkshire churches, especially from monumental inscriptions and stained glass.
WILSON, CHRISTOPHER, ed. *Medieval art and architecture in the East Riding of Yorkshire.* British Archaeological Association conference transactions for the year 1983. 9. 1989. Contents include, amongst other essays, GITTOS, BRIAN, &

GITTOS, MARY. 'A survey of East Riding sepulchral monuments to 1500'; DAWTON, NICHOLAS, 'The Percy tomb workshop'; BADHAM, SALLY, 'Monumental brasses: the development of the York workshops in the fourteenth and fifteenth centuries', *etc.* 'Curious epitaphs', *Y.N.Q.II. passim.*

Brasses

STEPHENSON, MILL. 'Monumental brasses in the East Riding', *Y.A.J.* 12, 1893, 195-229. See also 14, 1896-7, 507-13.
LAWRANCE, HENRY. 'Monumental brasses in the East Riding of Yorkshire', *Y.A.J.* 27, 1924, 380-87. At Brantingham, Cherry Burton, Little Driffield, Hull, Hunmanby, Londesborough, Patrington, Stillingfleet and Sutton on Derwent.
STEPHENSON, MILL. 'Monumental brasses in the North Riding', *Y.A.J.* 17, 1902-3, 261-339.
STEPHENSON, MILL. 'Monumental brasses in the West Riding,' *Y.A.J.* 15, 1900, 1-60.
STEPHENSON, MILL. 'Monumental brasses in Yorkshire: some additions and corrections', *Y.A.J.* 20, 1908-9, 291-317.
'List of Yorkshire brasses' *Old Yorkshire* 2, 1881, 59-61.

Effigies

ROUTH, PAULINE E. *Medieval effigial alabaster tombs in Yorkshire.* Ipswich: Boydell Press, 1976.
I'ANSON, WILLIAM M. *Some Yorkshire effigies',* *Y.A.J.* 27, 1924, 117-39.
I'ANSON, WILLIAM M. 'The mediaeval military effigies of Yorkshire', *Y.A.J.* 28, 1926, 345-79; 29, 1929, 1-67. Discussion.

Heraldry

BLOOM, J. HARVEY. *The heraldry in the churches of the West Riding of Yorkshire.* 6 vols. Hemsworth: C.E. Turner, 1892-5. Reference should be made to volume 6 of this bibliography for works on grants of arms, *etc.* Inscriptions in particular churches are listed below.

Hatchments

SUMMERS, PETER. *Hatchments in Britain 3: the Northern counties: Cumberland, Westmorland, Durham, Northumberland, Lancashire and Yorkshire.* Phillimore, 1980.

Out of County Inscriptions

'Monumental inscriptions from other counties relating to Yorkshire', *Y.C.M.* 1-2, 1891-2, *passim*.

'London gravestone inscriptions respecting Yorkshire people', *Y.G.* 2, 1890, 181-3.

TAYLOR, R.V. 'Yorkshire dead in Westminster Abbey,' *Old Yorkshire* 3, 1882, 81-90. List with brief biographical notes, 1596-1879.

B. Local Collections of Inscriptions

Addingham

CLAYTON, BRIAN. *Addingham St. Peter's memorial inscriptions.* [Leeds]: Wharfedale F.H.G., [1997].

CLAYTON, BRIAN. *Addingham Wesleyan memorial inscriptions.* [Leeds]: Family History Group, 1997.

CLAYTON, BRIAN. 'Addingham war memorial', *Wh.N.* 26, 1997, 25. List of men commemorated for 1914-18 and 1939-45.

Adel

Monumental inscriptions at the parish church of St. John the Baptist, Adel. Leeds: Wharfedale Family History Group, 1998.

Aldborough

LEADMAN, ALEX D.H. 'Aldborough church, near Boroughbridge', *Y.A.J.* 9, 1886, 163-96 & 303-20. Include monumental inscriptions, extracts from the parish register, list of clergy, *etc.*

Aldbrough

Monumental inscriptions: Aldbrough. E.Y.F.H.S., M.I. 25. 1988.

Aldfield

GRAINGER, K., & MORTON, O. *Monumental inscriptions from the villages of Aldfield - St. Lawrence the Martyr; Studley Royal - St. Mary's; Sawley - St. Michael and All Angels; Skelton-on-Ure - Christ the Consoler - Methodist - St. Helen's.* [ ]: Ripon & Harrogate Family History Group, 1996.

Ardsley

See Doncaster Archdeaconry

Arkendale

See Farnham

Arksey

See Bentley

Arthington

CHALKER, WYN. *Arthington St. Peters memorial inscriptions.* [Leeds]: Wharfedale Family History Group, [1997].

Askrigg

'War memorials: St. Oswald's church, Askrigg', *J.Cl.F.H.S.* 7(4), 1998, 65.

Atwick

Atwick monumental inscriptions. E.Y.F.H.S., 1996.

Aysgarth

ABRAHAM, EVELYN, & KIRBY, MARIAN. *Monumental inscriptions, Aysgarth in Wensleydale, North Yorkshire.* 2 vols. Bishopdale booklet 27-8. Bishopdale: Bishopdale Archives, 1992. Not seen.

Badsworth

BUCHANAN, SHARON. *Monumental inscriptions of St. Mary the Virgin, Badsworth, in the West Riding of Yorkshire.* Pontefract: Pontefract & District F.H.S., 1998.

Bainton

Monumental inscriptions, Bainton. E.Y.F.H.S., M.I. 74, 1995.

Barmston

Barmston and Harpham monumental inscriptions [ ]: E.Y.F.H.S., M.I. 95. 1997.

Barnoldswick

Lancashire monumental inscriptions: Barnoldswick St. Mary Le Gill church. B38. 2 fiche. [ ]: Lancashire Family History & Heraldry Society, 1991. Actually in Yorkshire.

Beamsley

See Harrogate

Beeford

Beeford, Dunnington and Lissett monumental inscriptions. E.Y.F.H.S., 1996.

Bentley
Monumental inscriptions not previously recorded: Bentley with Arksey. Doncaster: Doncaster & District F.H.S., 1998.

Bessingby
See North Grimston

Beswick
Monumental inscriptions: Beswick. E.Y.F.H.S., M.I. **76**. 1994.

Beverley
Beverley Minster (St. John & St. Martin) monumental inscriptions. [ ]: E.Y.F.H.S., 1997.
BOULTER, W. CONSITT. 'On three epitaphs in Beverley Minster', Y.A.J. **1**, 1870, 331-4.
Beverley St. Mary's, including Coronation Gardens: monumental inscriptions. [ ]: E.Y.F.H.S., M.I. **83**; 1995.

Bilton
Bilton monumental inscriptions. E.Y.F.H.S., M.I. **67**. 1993.
See also Harrogate

Bingley
JOHNSTONE, CHRISTINE. 'Monumental inscriptions at Bingley parish church,' K.D.F.H.S.J. Autumn 1996. 7-8. Surnames only.

Bishop Burton
WALFORD, ENID, & WALFORD, WALTER, et al. Bishop Burton monumental inscriptions. E.Y.F.H.S., M.I. **8**. 1985.

Bishop Wilton
Bishop Wilton monumental inscriptions. E.Y.F.H.S., M.I. **52**. 1991.

Blackley
Baptist Church, Blackley, monumental inscriptions. [ ]: Calderdale F.H.S., [199-?]

Blacktoft
Monumental inscriptions: Blacktoft. E.Y.F.H.S., M.I. **71**. 1994.

Bolling Hall
PRIEST, SYLVIA C. 'Armorial glass at Bolling Hall', B.A. **10**; N.S. **8**, 1962, 182-96.

Booth
SUTCLIFFE, JOHN. Booth United Reformed Church monumental inscriptions. [ ]: Calderdale F.H.S., 1993.

Bradford
SEWELL, A.B., & THORNTON, JOHN. 'Copies of inscriptions from monuments on the north side of the chancel in the parish church, Bradford', B.A. **1**, 1888, 51-2, 107-9 & 233-4.
THORNTON, JOHN. 'Local heraldry, with examples from the Bradford parish church', B.A. **2**, 1895, 277-86.
'Names taken from funeral silks and cards donated by Mr. W. Kipling, Bod-kin **33**, 1993, 4-5. Early 20th c.
'City of Bradford: Kirkgate Chapel burial ground removal of remains, Sept. 1897.' Bod-kin **27**, 1992, 5. List of 19th c. burials.

Bradshaw
BRAMBLES, TERRY, et al. St. John's church, Bradshaw, monumental inscriptions. [ ]: Calderdale F.H.S., 1994.

Brantingham
Brantingham and Ellerker monumental inscriptions. E.Y.F.H.S., M.I. **13**. 1986.

Bridlington Priory
Bridlington Priory monumental inscriptions. 2 pts. Cottingham: E.Y.F.H.S., 1996.

Broomfleet
See Cave

Buckrose Deanery
COLLIER, C.V., & LAWRANCE, HENRY. 'Ancient heraldry in the Deanery of Buckrose', Y.A.J. **24**, 1906-7, 383-95.

Bulmer Deanery
LAWRANCE, HENRY, & COLLIER, C.V. 'Ancient heraldry in the Deanery of Bulmer', Y.A.J. **27**, 1924, 140-65.

Burgh Wallis
See Doncaster Deanery

Burley in Wharfedale
ASCOUGH, GWEN, & OLIVER, IVY. Burley in Wharfedale: God's Acre Cemetery monumental inscriptions. Leeds: Wharfedale Family History Group, 1998.

Burnt Yates
See Killinghall

Burstwick
Burstwick monumental inscriptions.
E.Y.F.H.S., M.I. **82**. 1994.

Burton Agnes
Burton Agnes and Ruston Parva monumental inscriptions. E.Y.F.H.S., M.I. **82**. 1994.

Calwick
Calwick monumental inscriptions. E.Y.F.H.S., M.I. **17**. 1987.

Carlton
Monumental inscriptions of the burial grounds of Carlton juxta Snaith, incorporating Carlton Cemetery, St.Mary's parish church, & St. Mary's Catholic Church. Fiche. Doncaster: Doncaster & District F.H.S., 199-? Not seen.

Catterick Deanery
COLLIER, C.V., & LAWRANCE, H. 'Ancient heraldry in the Deanery of Catterick', *Y.A.J.* **29**, 1929, 202-24. Includes folded pedigrees of Langton, medieval-18th c., and Lisle, 13- 16th c.

Cherry Burton
Cherry Burton monumental inscriptions. E.Y.F.H.S., M.I. **21**. [1988?]

Cleveland Deanery
See Ryedale Deanery

Conisborough
RAINE, [J]. 'On some early monuments of Conisborough', *Reports and papers of the Associated Architectural Societies* **9**(1), 1867, 69-74. Mainly extracts from wills.

Conistone
MARSDEN, WENDY. *Conistone St. Mary memorial inscriptions.* [Leeds]: Wharfedale Family History Group, [1997].

Copley
MONTGOMERY, JANET, et al. *St. Stephens, Copley monumental inscriptions.* [ ]: Calderdale F.H.S., 1994.

Cottingham
HARVEY, A.S. 'Cottingham church and its heraldry', *Y.A.J.* **40**, 1962, 265-97. Includes pedigrees of Stuteville and Wake, and of Holand, Earls of Kent, medieval.
STAMP, A.H. *In memoriam: a survey of the churchyard and church of St. Mary's, Cottingham.* Cottingham local history series **12**. Cottingham: Cottingham Local History Society, 1991.
Cottingham monumental inscriptions E.Y.F.H.S., M.I. **58**. 1992.

Cotton Stones
BRAMBLES, TERRY, et al. *St. Mary's Cotton Stones, monumental inscriptions.* [ ]: Calderdale F.H.S., 1994.

Dacre
OLIVER, ALAN. *Monumental inscriptions from the villages of Dacre: Providence Chapel U.R.C., Dacre Banks - Holy Trinity.* 1 fiche, [ ]: Ripon and Harrogate Family History Group, 1996.

Dallowgill
See West Tanfield

Danby
'In memoriam', *J.Cl.F.H.S.* **5**(3), 1992. 17-20. List of a collection of 'in memoriam' cards for the Danby and Glaisdale area, 19-20th c.

Darfield
See Doncaster Archdeaconry

Darley
See Greenhow Hill

Delph
LAMBERT, HOWARD. 'Monumental inscriptions at Delph Independent Chapel', *B.S.H.S.* **24**(1), 1994, 4-12; **24**(2), 1994, 16-19; **25**(3), 1995, 19-25; **26**(2), 1996, 14-18; **27**(2), 1997, 8- 13; **28**(4), 1998, 16-21. 300 inscriptions.
SMITH, J. 'In memory of: gravestone inscriptions at St. Thomas's church, Heights, Delph, recalling inhabitants of Hollinbank', *B.S.H.S.* **20**(4), 1990-91, 11.

Denton

MITCHELL, FRANK. *Denton St. Helen's memorial inscriptions.* [Leeds]: Wharfedale Family History Group, [1997].

Dickering Deanery

COLLIER, C.V., & LAWRANCE, HENRY. 'Ancient heraldry in the Deanery of Dickering', *Y.A.J.* **25**, 1908-9, 71-90.

Doncaster. Hyde Park

Hyde Park Cemetery monumental inscriptions. 12 fiche. Doncaster: Doncaster & District F.H.S., [199-]. Not seen. Cemetery in Doncaster.

Doncaster Archdeaconry

Monumental inscriptions taken from churches & churchyards within the Archdeaconry of Doncaster. 12 sets of fiche. Doncaster & District F.H.S., [199-?]. Not seen.

Index of surnames found in the churches and churchyards of the Archdeaconry of Doncaster, includes: Goole, Ardsley, Darfield, Tickhill, and surrounding areas. Doncaster: Doncaster Society for Family History, 1990.

Doncaster Deanery

FAIRBANK, F.R. 'Ancient memorial brasses remaining in the old Deanery of Doncaster', *Y.A.J.* **11**, 1892, 71-94. From the churches of Rotherham, Rawmarsh, Sprotborough, Todwick, Marr, Owston and Burgh Wallis; includes pedigrees of Swift of Rotherham 16-17th c., Darley of Buttercrambe, 16th c., Fitzwilliam of Sprotborough, 15th c., *etc.*

Draughton

CLAYTON, BRIAN, ed. *Draughton Wesleyan Methodist Chapel: a brief history of the chapel with the memorial inscriptions & abstract of the burial register, 1847-1956.* [ ]: Wharfedale Family History Group, 1997.

Driffield

Driffield monumental inscriptions. E.Y.F.H.S., M.I. **34**. 1989.

Dunnington

See Beeford

Easington

MOUNT, DAVID. *Easington monumental inscriptions.* E.Y.F.H.S., M.I. **7**. 1984.

East Ardsley

BEDFORD, ERIC. *Monumental inscriptions: parish church of St. Michael, East Ardsley.* 2 fiche. [Morley]: Morley and District F.H.S., [1995].

Eastrington

Eastrington monumental inscriptions. Cottingham: E.Y.F.H.S., 1997.

Ecclesfield

DRURY, CHARLES. 'Notes on some remains of ancient heraldic glass and other heraldry in Ecclesfield church', *T.Hunter A.S.* **1**(3-4), 1918, 331-6.

Elland

CLAY, JOHN WILLIAM. 'Elland church', *Y.A.J.* **10**, 1889, 104-16 & 205-16. Monumental inscriptions.

Ellerker

See Brantingham

Ellerton

Ellerton M.I's. E.Y.F.H.S., M.I. **22**. 1988.

Elloughton

Elloughton M.I's. E.Y.F.H.S., M.I. **16**. 1987.

Escrick

CLARK, YVONNE. *Escrick monumental inscriptions.* E.Y.F.H.S., M.I. **54**. 1991.

Everingham

See North Grimston

Farnham

OLIVER, ALAN. *Monumental inscriptions. Farnham, Scotton; Staveley; Arkendale.* 1 fiche. [ ]: Ripon & Harrogate Family History Group, 1995.

Felixkirk

'On the heraldry at Feliskirk,' *Y.A.J.* **22**, 1913, 198-203. Includes pedigree of Cantilupe.

Fewston

ASCOUGH, GWEN, & OLIVER, IVY. *Fewston, Meagill Lane Cemetery memorial inscriptions.* Leeds: Wharfedale Family History Group, 1998.

Filey

JACKSON, CHARLES. 'Church notes taken at Filey, Yorkshire, 29 July 1876', *M.G.H.* N.S., 2, 1877, 552-3 & 573-5.

Folkton

Folkton monumental inscriptions. Cottingham: E.Y.F.H.S., 1998.

Foston on the Wolds

Monumental inscriptions, Foston on the Wolds. E.Y.F.H.S., M.I. 81. 1994.

Fountains

GILYARD-BEER, R. 'The graves of the abbots of Fountains', *Y.A.J.* 59, 1987, 45-50. List.

Fountains Hall

MURRAY, HUGH. 'The heraldic window at Fountains Hall', *Y.A.J.* 62, 1990, 171-86. Includes pedigrees of Proctor, 16-17th c., and Mereworth.

Ganton

Ganton monumental inscriptions. Cottingham: E.Y.F.H.S., 1997.

Garton

See Tunstall

Gisburn

Memorial inscriptions, St. Mary's, Gisburn. 2 fiche. G5. [ ]: Lancashire Family History and Heraldry Society, 1982.

Glaisdale

See Danby

Goodmanham

Goodmanham monumental inscriptions. E.Y.F.H.S., M.I. 48. 1991.

Goole

Goole Cemetery monumental inscriptions. 2 vols. Boothferry Family and Local History Group, 1998. Not seen.
See also Doncaster Archdeaconry

Goxhill

See Hornsea

Greenhow Hill

OLIVER, ALAN, & CLOVER, JOHN. *Monumental inscriptions, burial register, St. Mary's, & Wayside Cemetery, Greenhow Hill. Books of remembrance - Darley & Thornthwaite.* [ ]: Ripon Historical Society, 1996. Includes burial register of Greenhow Hill, 1858-1996.

Grewellthorpe

See Ripon

Grindleton

FARROW, DOROTHY, et al. *Grindleton Methodist Free Church, Grindleton: monumental inscriptions.* G6. 1 fiche. [ ]: Lancashire Family History and Heraldry Society, Ribble Valley Branch, 1990.
St. Ambrose parish church, Grindleton: monumental inscriptions. G7. 1 fiche. [ ]: Lancashire Family History and Heraldry Society, Ribble Valley Branch, 1989.

Guiseley

ARMYTAGE, GEORGE JOHN. 'Monumental inscriptions: St. Oswald's church, Guiseley, Yorkshire', *Y.A.J.* 6, 1881, 80-91.

Hackness

Hackness monumental inscriptions. [ ]: E.Y.F.H.S., 1996.

Halifax

BRETTON, R. 'The heraldry of the Halifax parish church,' *T.Hal.A.S.* 1931, 29-72. Notes from monumental inscriptions.
CROSSLEY, E.W. *The monumental and other inscriptions in Halifax parish church.* Leeds: John Whitehead & Son, 1909.
BRAMBLES, TERRY. et al. *Society of Friends, Quaker Meeting House, Clare Road, Halifax, monumental inscriptions.* [ ]: Calderdale F.H.S., 1990.
BRETTON, R. 'Pellon Lane Baptist graveyard inscriptions', *T.Hal.A.S.* 1952, 86-94. In Halifax.

Halsham

Halsham monumental inscriptions. E.Y.F.H.S., M.I. 56. 1992.

Hampsthwaite

See Harrogate

Harewood

ROUTH, PAULINE, & KNOWLES, RICHARD. *The medieval monuments of Harewood.* Wakefield: Wakefield Historical Publications, 1983. Includes pedigrees of Gascoigne of Gawthorpe, also of the lords of Harewood, with wills of Sir William Gascoigne, Bt., 1419, Sir Richard Redman, 1425 and Edmond Redman, 1510.

Harpham

See Barmston

Harrogate

OLIVER, ALAN, et al. *Monumental inscriptions: High Harrogate; Christ Church, Harrogate; St. John (Bilton); St. Peter; St. Wilfred.* 2 fiche. [ ]. Ripon and Harrogate Family History Group, 1995.

OLIVER, ALAN. *Monumental inscriptions: Methodist chapels. Harrogate Circuit; Gracious Street, Knaresborough; Beamsley; West Tanfield.* 1 fiche. [ ]: Ripon & Harrogate Family History Group, 1995. Harrogate Circuit includes Wesley Chapel, Harrogate; and the chapels at Harlow Hill, Harrogate; West End Park, Harrogate; Oatlands Mount, Harrogate; Grove Road, Harrogate; Hampsthwaite; Killinghall; Wetherby Road, Harrogate; Starbeck; Bar Methodist Church, Harrogate; and Pannal.

Harthill Deanery

COLLIER, C.V., & LAWRANCE, HENRY. 'Ancient heraldry in the Deanery of Harthill', *Y.A.J.* **26**, 1922, 93-143.

Hawksworth

HARTLEY, JOHN. *Hawksworth Methodist Church memorial inscriptions.* Leeds: Wharfedale Family History Group, 1998.

Hebden Bridge

BRAMBLES, TERRY, et al. *Cross Lanes United Methodist Church, Hebden Bridge, monumental inscriptions.* [ ]: Calderdale F.H.S., 1991.

Hedon

St. Augustine's church, Hedon, monumental inscriptions. E.Y.F.H.S., M.I. **51**. 1991.

Heptonstall

BRETTON, R. 'Local funeral hatchments', *T.Hal.A.S.* 1952, 43-7. At Heptonstall and Sowerby.

Hessle

Hessle monumental inscriptions. E.Y.F.H.S., M.I. **59**. 1992.

Hickleton

WHITING, C.E. 'The heraldry of Hickleton church', *T.Hunter A.S.* **5**, 1943, 173-82.

High Harrogate

See Harrogate

Hilston

See Tunstall

Hipperholme

MORGAN, LESLIE. 'Little-known graveyards', *T.Hal.A.S.* 1971, 33-8. Inscription from Hipperholme Wesleyan Methodist graveyard.

Holderness Deanery

LAWRANCE, HENRY, & COLLIER, C.V. 'Ancient heraldry in the Deanery of Holderness', *Y.A.J.* **26**, 1922, 230-50.

Hollym

MOUNT, DAVE, ed. *Hollym monumental inscriptions.* E.Y.F.H.S., M.I. **55**. 1991.

Holmpton

Holmpton monumental inscriptions. E.Y.F.H.S., M.I. **49**. 1991.

Holywell Green

SUTCLIFFE, JOHN. *Holywell Green United Reformed Church: monumental inscriptions and burial register details.* [ ]: Calderdale F.H.S., 1993.

Honley

'Honley church', *Y.C.M.* **2**, 1892, 5-10. Includes 'monumental tablets placed within the church', and extracts from chapel wardens' accounts, 1791-1828.

Hornsea

Hornsea and Goxhill monumental inscriptions. [ ]: E.Y.F.H.S., 1996.

Horsforth

WOLSTENHULME, LES. 'The Horsforth boulder stone', *Wh.N.* **22**, 1996, 16-18; **23**, 1997, 6-8. Memorial to Horsforth people killed in the Great War; lists 211 names.

WOLSTENHULME, LES, & CLAYTON, BRIAN. *Cragg Hill Baptist Church, Horsforth (formerly Horsforth Zion Baptist Chapel) memorial inscriptions (1809-1948).* Leeds: Wharfedale Family History Group, 1998.

Hotham

Hotham monumental inscriptions. E.Y.F.H.S., M.I. **14**. 1986.

Howden

FAIRBANK, F.R. 'Memorial brasses in Howden church', *Y.A.J.* **11**, 1891, 170-3. Includes pedigree of Dolman, 17th c.

Huddersfield

WHITWAM, STEPHEN D. *Huddersfield parish church grave yard inscriptions.* Huddersfield: H. & D.F.H.S., 1993.

Huggate

Huggate monumental inscriptions. Cottingham: E.Y.F.H.S., 1998.

Hull

Air Street

Air St., Hull monumental inscriptions. E.Y.F.H.S., M.I. **35**. 1990.

Castle Street

MOUNT, DAVID, ed. *Castle Street M.I.s: burial ground for Holy Trinity church, Hull.* E.Y.F.H.S., M.I. **9**. 1985.

TROWSDALE, T.B. *A visit to the old burial ground in Castle Street, Hull.* Hull: J.M. Taylor, 1878. Reprinted from the *Hull Miscellany.* Reprinted in Malet Lambert local history reprints 7. Hull: Malet Lambert High School, 1980.

'Castle Street Burial Ground', *B.T.* **52**, 1992, 33. Brief note on inscriptions in a Hull cemetery, 19th c.

Holy Trinity

Hull Holy Trinity (churchyard only) monumental inscriptions. Cottingham: E.Y.F.H.S., 1997.

TASKER, JOHN HOWARD. *Monumental inscriptions within the parish church of the Most Holy, Blessed and Undivided Trinity, Kingston upon Hull, together with divers other inscriptions within the church.* Malet Lambert local history originals **29**. Hull: Malet Lambert, 1985.

WALTER, D. ALLEYNE. 'The armorial ledger stones in the church of the Holy Trinity, Hull', *Reliquary* N.S., **2**, 1888, 129-32 & 215; **3**, 1889, 41-2, 89-90 & 168.

WALTER, ALLEYNE. 'Inscriptions on armorial ledger stones, Holy Trinity church, Hull', *M.G.H.* 2nd series **1**, 1886, 140 & 172.

St. Mary, Lowgate

TASKER, JOHN HOWARD. *Monumental inscriptions within the church of St. Mary, Lowgate, Kingston upon Hull, also within the churchyard and within the burial ground at Trippet, together with divers other inscriptions within the church.* Malet Lambert local history originals **16**. Hull: Malet Lambert High School, 1983.

Humbleton

Monumental inscriptions, Humbleton. E.Y.F.H.S., M.I. **38**. 1990.

Hutton Rudby

'Memorial board at Hutton Rudby', *J.Cl.F.H.S.* **6**(1), 1995, 31-2. Memorial (probably) to members of a benevolent society, 19th c.

Hyde Park

See Doncaster. Hyde Park

Idle

TURNER, J. HORSFALL, ed. *Idle Upper Chapel burial registers and graveyard inscriptions, with notices of the Quaker burial ground, Westfield Lane, and of the private burial ground, Thackley End.* Bingley: Harrison and Sons, [1906.] Nonconformist monumental inscriptions.

Ilkley
CLAYTON, BRIAN, ed. *Ilkley All Saints parish church memorial inscriptions*. Leeds: Wharfedale Family History Group, 1998.
PAYNE, JOHN ORLEBAR, ed. 'Inscriptions from Middleton Hall chapel, Ilkley, Yorkshire', in *Miscellanea* **4**. C.R.S. **4**, 1907, 429-30.

Ingleby Arncliffe
BROWN, WILLIAM. 'Heraldic glass from Ingleby Arncliffe and Kirby Sigston churches', *Y.A.J.* **22**, 1913, 137-44. Includes pedigree of Ryhill.

Keighley. Utley Cemetery
Monumental inscriptions at Utley Cemetery. 5 vols to date. Keighley & District F.H.S. 1995- . Not seen.
'Locations extracted from monumental inscriptions at Utley Cemetery, Keighley', *K.D.F.H.S.J.* Autumn 1994, 19-20.

Keyingham
Keyingham & Thorngumbald monumental inscriptions. E.Y.F.H.S., M.I. **29**. 1989.

Killinghall
OLIVER, ALAN, et al. *Monumental inscriptions: Killinghall; Burnt Yates; Padside; Ramsgill.* 1 fiche. [ ]: Ripon & Harrogate Family History Group, 1995.
See also Harrogate

Kilnsea
See Skeffling

Kilnwick
Monumental inscriptions, Kilnwick. E.Y.F.H.S., M.I. **73**. 1994.

Kipping
WALSH, JOSIE. 'Arthur Blackburn's memorial inscriptions: Kipping Congregational Chapel, Thornton', *Bod-kin* **26**, 1992, 14. Index to inscriptions.

Kirby Sigston
See Ingleby Arncliffe

Kirk Ella
Kirk Ella monumental inscriptions. E.Y.F.H.S., M.I. **64**. 1992.

Kirkby Malzeard
HEBDEN, J., GRAINGER, K., & MORTON, O. *Monumental inscriptions from the villages of Kirkby Malzeard: St. Andrew, Kirkby Malzeard; Cemetery; Mickley, St. John the Evangelist.* 1 fiche. [ ]: Ripon & Harrogate Family History Group, 1996.

Kirkthorpe
WHITTLE, ERIC S. 'The Benedictine burials in Kirkthorpe churchyard', *Wakefield Historical Society journal* **2**, 1975, 41-2. List of nuns' burials, 1811-20.

Knaresborough
See Harrogate

Laxton
Monumental inscriptions, Laxton. E.Y.F.H.S., M.I. **68**. 1993.

Leavening
WADDINGTON, ROGER. 'Quakers and the burial ground', *Yorkshire history quarterly* **2**(2), 1996, 81-2. At Leavening; brief history of the cemetery.

Leeds
LUMB, G.D. 'Monuments in S. John's Church, Leeds', in *Miscellanea* **[10]**. *T.S.* **33**, 1935, 306-426.
RUSBY, JAMES. 'Hunter's church notes', *Miscellanea* **1**. *T.S.* **2**. 1891, 26-35. Monumental inscriptions at St. Peter's and St. John's, Leeds.
'Leeds parish church: inscriptions on the tombstones in the churchyard', in *Miscellanea* **[7]**. *T.S.* **24**, 1919, 256-76; *Miscellanea* **[8]**. *T.S.* **26**, 1924, 41-60.

Leven
Leven, St. Faith's monumental inscriptions. E.Y.F.H.S., M.I. **39**. 1990.
Leven (St. Faith's and Holy Trinity) monumental inscriptions. Cottingham: E.Y.F.H.S., 1997.

Lissett
See Beeford

Lockington
Lockington monumental inscriptions. E.Y.F.H.S., M.I. **4**. 1983.

Long Preston
Parish church of St. Mary the Virgin, Long Preston: monumental inscriptions. L5. 2 fiche. [ ]: Lancaster Family History and Heraldry Society, Ribble Valley Branch, 1989.

Long Riston
Long Riston monumental inscriptions. E.Y.F.H.S., M.I. 28. 1989.

Lowerton
See Oxenhope. Lowerton

Lowthorpe
WOLEDGE, LESLEY, ed. *Lowthorpe monumental inscriptions.* E.Y.F.H.S., M.I. 3. 1982.

Luddenden Foot
BRAMBLES, TERRY, et al. *St. Mary's, Luddenden Foot, monumental inscriptions.* [ ]: Calderdale F.H.S., 1996.
POLLARD, DAVID, WILDE, MARGARET, & CLYNE, MARGARET. *Denholme United Methodist Church, Luddenden Foot, monumental inscriptions.* [ ]: Calderdale F.H.S., 1995.

Lund
Lund monumental inscriptions. E.Y.F.H.S., M.I. 5. 1983.

Mappleton
Mappleton monumental inscriptions. E.Y.F.H.S., M.I. 20. 1988.

Marfleet
Marfleet monumental inscriptions. E.Y.F.H.S., M.I. 65. 1993.

Market Weighton
Market Weighton monumental inscriptions. E.Y.F.H.S., M.I. 66. 1993.

Marr
See Doncaster Deanery

Marske
RAINE, JAMES. 'Marske, in Swaledale', *Y.A.J.* 6, 1881, 172-286. Includes inscriptions, list of rectors, and many pedigrees.

Menston
JOHNSON, KEN. *Menston St. John memorial inscriptions.* [Leeds]: Wharfedale Family History Group, 1997.

Mickley
See Kirkby Malzeard

Middleton on the Wolds
CAWLEY, ANDREA, & CAWLEY, MARTIN. *Middleton on the Wolds.* E.Y.F.H.S., M.I. 6. 1983.

Middleton Tyas
SAYWELL, J.L. 'Parochial history: Middleton Tyas', *Y.C.M.* 1, 1891, 114-20. Monumental inscriptions.

Midgley
DUNFORD, RITA, et al. *Providence United Methodist Church, Midgley, monumental inscriptions.* [ ]: Calderdale F.H.S., 1995.

Milnsbridge
BALL, KENNETH. *Milnsbridge Baptist Church grave yard inscriptions.* Huddersfield: H. & D.F.H.S., 1990.

Mixenden
DAWSON, MARY, et al. *Moor End United Reformed Church, Mount Tabor.* [ ]: Calderdale F.H.S., 1998. Monumental inscriptions at Mixenden.

Morley
SMITH, WILLIAM. 'The graveyard at Morley Old Chapel', *Old Yorkshire* 1, 1891, 111-16. Includes notes on inscriptions.
SMITH, WILLIAM. 'Monumental inscriptions in the graveyard of St. Mary's in the Wood, Morley, W.R. Yorkshire', *M.G.H.* N.S., 3, 1880, 306-8, 331-2 & 343-4.
'Morley war memorial, 1914-1918', *Cameo* 1994, no.3, 19-20; 1995, no.1, 14-15.

Mottram
See York

Mount Pellon
TOWN, JAMES, & TOWN, DORIS. *Christ Church, Mount Pellon monumental inscriptions and burial register details.* 7 fiche. [ ]: Calderdale F.H.S., 1995. Includes burials, 1854-1973. The register has been used to annotate inscriptions.

Mytholmroyd
JOHNYS, BARBARA, BRAMBLES, TERRY, &
WILDE, MARGARET. *Mytholmroyd
Wesleyan Methodist Church monumental
inscriptions.* [ ]: Calderdale F.H.S., 1993.
BRAMBLES, TERRY, et al. *St. Michaels church,
Mytholmroyd, monumental incriptions.*
[ ]: Calderdale F.H.S., 1995.

Naburn
Monumental inscriptions: Naburn.
E.Y.F.H.S., M.I. 72. 1994.

Norland
*Mount Zion Primitive Methodist Chapel,
Norland: monumental inscriptions.*
Calderdale F.H.S., 1993.

Normanton
TOMLINSON, GEO. W. 'On monuments in
Normanton church, with genealogical
notes', *Y.A.J.* 5, 1879, 267-88.

North Cave
North Cave M.I.'s. E.Y.F.H.S., M.I. 15. 1986.

North Dalton
Monumental inscriptions, North Dalton.
Cottingham: E.Y.F.H.S., 1997.

North Ferriby
North Ferriby monumental inscriptions.
E.Y.F.H.S., M.I. 18. 1987.

North Frodingham
North Frodingham monumental inscriptions.
E.Y.F.H.S., M.I. 1. [1982?]

North Grimston
STEPHENSON, MILL. 'Some additional brasses
in the East Riding', *Y.A.J.* 24, 1917, 269-
74. From North Grimston, Norton-next-
Malton, Settrington, Everingham and
Bessingby.

North Newbald
Monumental inscriptions North Newbald.
E.Y.F.H.S., M.I. 77. 1994.

North Stainley
See Ripon

Norton
See North Grimston

Ottringham
Ottringham monumental inscriptions.
E.Y.F.H.S., M.I. 61. 1992.

Ovenden
BRAMBLES, TERRY, et al. *Nursery Lane
Wesleyan Methodist Church, Ovenden,
monumental inscriptions.* [ ]: Calderdale
F.H.S., 1992.

Owston
See Doncaster Deanery

Oxenhope

Horkinstone
*Monumental inscriptions and burial
register at Horkinstone Baptist Chapel,
Oxenhope, near Keighley.* Keighley:
Keighley Family History Publishing,
1997.

Lowerton
KINGHORN, DORINDA S. 'The old Methodist
burial ground at Lowerton, Oxenhope,
Keighley', *K.D.F.H.S.J.* Summer 1991, 13-14.
General description, with note on the
author's transcript.
'Lowertown old burial ground', *K.D.F.H.S.J.*
Summer 1993, 14-15. See also Summer 1994,
13; Spring 1996, 11-12. General discussion,
with notes on Baldwin, Whalley, Beaver
and Bancroft families.

Padside
See Killinghall

Pannal
See Harrogate

Patrington
Patrington monumental inscriptions.
E.Y.F.H.S., M.I. 62. 1992.

Paull
Paull monumental inscriptions. E.Y.F.H.S.,
M.I. 63. 1992.

Pecketwell
Crimsworth Methodist Church, Pecketwell, monumental inscriptions. [ ]: Calderdale F.H.S., 1994.

Pellon Lane
See Halifax

Pocklington
LEADMAN, ALEX D.H. 'Pocklington church', *Y.A.J.* **14**, 1896-7, 85-132. Includes monumental inscriptions, list of vicars, extracts from parish registers, list of wills, *etc.*

Preston
Preston monumental inscriptions. E.Y.F.H.S., M.I. 30. 1989.

Ramsgill
See Killinghall

Rawdon Cragg
PRATT, CHRISTINE. *Rawdon Cragg Baptist memorial inscriptions.* Wharfedale Family History Group, 1997.

Rawmarsh
See Doncaster Deanery

Reighton
Reighton monumental inscriptions. [ ]: E.Y.F.H.S., M.I. 85. 1996.

Richmond Deanery
See Ryedale Deanery

Ripon
WILSON, THOMAS. *A verbatim copy of all the monuments, gravestones & other sepulchral memorials in Ripon Cathedral and its burial ground.* Ripon: Wm. Harrison, 1847.
HEBDEN, JOHN, GRAINGER, K., & MORTON, O. *Monumental inscriptions. Ripon - Holy Trinity; Winkersley - St. Cuthbert & St. Oswald; North Stainley - St. Mary the Virgin.* 1 fiche. [ ]: Ripon & Harrogate Family History Group, 1998.

Rise
Rise monumental inscriptions. E.Y.F.H.S., M.I. 57. 1992.

Rotherham
See Doncaster Deanery

Routh
Routh monumental inscriptions. E.Y.F.H.S., M.I. 33. 1989.

Rowley
Rowley monumental inscriptions. E.Y.F.H.S., M.I. 32. 1989.

Rudston
Rudston monumental inscriptions. Cottingham: E.Y.F.H.S., 1997.

Ruston Parva
See Burton Agnes

Ryedale Deanery
LAWRANCE, HENRY, & COLLIER, C.V. 'Ancient heraldry in Yorkshire', *Y.A.J.* **28**, 1926, 34-79. For the Deaneries of Ryedale, Cleveland, and Richmond.

Salendine Nook
WHITWAM, STEPHEN DAVID, & WHITWAM, DIANE. *Salendine Nook Baptist Church ... graveyard inscriptions.* 2 vols. Huddersfield: H. & D.F.H.S., 1992.

Sancton
Monumental inscriptions, Sancton. E.Y.F.H.S., M.I. 75. 1994.

Sawley
See Aldfield

Scotton
See Farnham

Sculcoates
Sculcoates monumental inscriptions, north side. E.Y.F.H.S., M.I. 46. 1991.
Sculcoates monumental inscriptions, south side. E.Y.F.H.S., M.I. 47. 1991.

Seamer
Seamer monumental inscriptions. E.Y.F.H.S., M.I. 84. 1996.

Selby
RICHARDSON, A.W. 'Two fourteenth-century effigies in Selby Abbey church', *Y.A.J.* **38**, 1955, 246-56. Includes folded pedigree of Furnival, medieval.

Settle

JOHNSTONE, CHRISTINE. 'Monumental inscriptions', *K.D.F.H.S.J.* Autumn 1995, 23-4. At Friends Meeting House, Settle, 19-20th c.

Settrington

See North Grimston

Sheffield

GLASSBY, WILLIAM J.J. *The old churchyards of Sheffield, with a brief selection of quaint epitaphs therein.* Sheffield: Pawson and Brailsford, 1896.

COLLIER, CARUS VALE. 'Notes on the heraldry in the parish church of Sheffield', *Reliquary* N.S., **4**, 1890, 212-8.

BERRY, A.R. 'Monumental inscriptions and dedications in St.Paul's church, Kimberworth Road' *F.S.* **10**(3), 1990, 70-71; **10**(4), 1990, 99-100; **11**(1), 1990, 18.

Sigglesthorne

Sigglesthorne M.I.s. E.Y.F.H.S., M.I. **10**. 1986.

Silkstone

WHITAKER, T. 'From a large monument in Silkstone churchyard', *Y.F.H.* **14**(1), 1988, 12. Monument to 26 miners killed when a mine flooded in 1838.

Skeffling

Skeffling & Kilnsea monumental inscriptions. E.Y.F.H.S., M.I. **44**. 1990.

Skelton on Ure

See Aldfield

Skerne

WOLEDGE, LESLEY, ed. *Skerne monumental inscriptions.* E.Y.F.H.S., M.I. **2**. 1982

Skidby

Monumental inscriptions: Skidby. E.Y.F.H.S., M.I. **26**. 1988.

Skipsea

Skipsea and Ulrome monumental inscriptions. [ ]: E.Y.F.H.S., 1996.

Skirlaugh

Skirlaugh monumental inscriptions. E.Y.F.H.S., M.I. **23**. 1988.

Slaidburn

SLAIDBURN WOMENS INSTITUTE. *The parish church of St. Andrew, Slaidburn: monumental inscriptions.* **89**. 2 fiche. [ ]: Lancashire Family History and Heraldry Society, [199-?]

WHITWAM, STEPHEN DAVID. 'John and Sarah Bottomley's funeral cards', *H. & D.F.H.S.J.* **8**(4), 1995, 124-8. List of a collection of funeral cards from Slaithwaite area, late 19th-early 20th c.

Snainton

Snainton monumental inscriptions. E.Y.F.H.S., M.I. **94**. 1997.

South Cave

South Cave and Broomfleet monumental inscriptions. E.Y.F.H.S., M.I. **19**. [1988?]

South Dalton

Monumental inscriptions: Dalton. E.Y.F.H.S., M.I. **27**. 1988.

South Kilvington

BROWN, WILLIAM. 'On the heraldry at Kilvington', *Y.A.J.* **22**, 1913, 226-31. Includes will extracts, 15-16th c.

Sowerby

BRETTON, ROWLAND. 'Heraldry in a Sowerby church', *T.Hal.A.S.* 1964, 59-64.

BRAMBLES, TERRY, et al. *Boulderclough United Methodist Church, Sowerby, monumental inscriptions.* [ ]: Calderdale F.H.S., 1994.

BRAMBLES, TERRY, et al. *Sowerby Congregational Church monumental inscriptions.* [ ]: Calderdale F.H.S., 1992.

BRAMBLES, TERRY, et al. *St. George's Church, Sowerby, monumental inscriptions.* [ ]: Calderdale F.H.S., 1993.

BRAMBLES, TERRY, et al. *Rooley Lane Wesleyan Methodist Church, Sowerby, monumental inscriptions.* [ ]: Calderdale F.H.S., 1992.

See also Heptonstall

Sowerby Bridge

BRAMBLES, TERRY, et al. *Bolton Brow Wesleyan Methodist Church, Sowerby Bridge, monumental inscriptions.* [ ]: Calderdale F.H.S., 1991-2.

Sproatley
Sproatley monumental inscriptions.
E.Y.F.H.S., M.I. **50**. 1991.

Sprotborough
See Doncaster Deanery

Stainforth
Stainforth cemetery monumental inscriptions. Doncaster: Doncaster & District F.H.S., [199-?] Not seen.

Stainland
Providence Chapel, Beestonley Lane, Stainland: monumental inscriptions. 3 fiche. [ ]: Calderdale F.H.S., 1996. Congregational chapel (subsequently U.R.C.) opened 1814 and closed 1985.

Starbeck
See Harrogate

Staveley
See Farnham

Studley Royal
See Aldfield

Sunk Island
Sunk Island monumental inscriptions.
E.Y.F.H.S., M.I. **43**. [1990?]

Sutton on Hull
Sutton-on-Hull monumental inscriptions.
2 pts. E.Y.F.H.S., M.I. **70**. 1993.

Swine
Monumental inscriptions, Swine. E.Y.F.H.S., M.I. **80**. 1994.
'Swine', *B.T.* **13**, 1982, 8-9. Extract from *Commercial directory* 1823, and list of names on gravestones in Swine churchyard.

Thirsk
'On the heraldry at Thirsk', *Y.A.J.* **22**, 1913, 210-6.

Thorne
Monumental inscriptions not previously recorded: Thorne. Doncaster: Doncaster & District F.H.S., 1998.

Thorngumbald
See Keyingham

Thornthwaite
See Greenhow Hill

Thrybergh
B., T. 'Church notes from Thrybergh, Yorkshire', *Topographer* **3**, 1790, 291-4. Monumental inscriptions.

Tickhill
See Doncaster Archdeaconry

Tingley
SMITH, WILLIAM. 'Tingley burial ground', *Old Yorkshire* **1**, 1881, 106-8. Includes notes on inscriptions.

Todwick
See Doncaster Deanery

Tosside
Mount Sion Congregational Chapel, Tosside: monumental inscriptions. **T6**. 1 fiche. [ ]: Lancashire Family History and Heraldry Society, 1989.
The parish church of St. Bartholomew, Tosside: monumental inscriptions. **T5**. 1 fiche. [ ]: Lancashire Family History and Heraldry Society, 1989.

Tunstall
Tunstall, Hilston & Garton monumental inscriptions. E.Y.F.H.S., M.I. **31**. 1989.

Ulrome
See Skipsea

Walkington
Walkington monumental inscriptions.
E.Y.F.H.S., M.I. **11**. 1986.

Warley
BRAMBLES, TERRY, WILDE, MARGARET, & TOWN, JIM. *Butts Green Baptist Chapel, Warley, monumental inscriptions.* [ ]: Calderdale F.H.S., 1995.

Warter
Warter. E.Y.F.H.S., M.I. **45**. 1988.

Watton
Monumental inscriptions, Watton. E.Y.F.H.S., M.I. **69**. 1993.

Wawne
Wawne M.I.s. E.Y.F.H.S., M.I. **12**. 1986.

Weeton
HARTLEY, JOHN. *Weeton St. Barnabas memorial inscriptions.* [Leeds]: Wharfedale Family History Group, [1997].

Welton
Welton monumental inscriptions. E.Y.F.H.S., M.I. **53**. [1991?]

Welwick
Welwick monumental inscriptions. E.Y.F.H.S., M.I. **60**. 1990.

West Tanfield
GRAINGER, K., MORTON, O., & HEBDEN, JOHN. *Monumental inscriptions: West Tanfield - St. Nicholas; Grewellthorpe - St. James; Dallowgill - St. Peter & Church of Resurrection.* [ ]: Ripon Historical Society, 1998.
See also Harrogate

Wharram Percy
RAHTZ, PHILIP, & WATTS, LORNA. *Wharram Percy: the memorial stones of the churchyard.* York University Archaeological publications 1. York: University of York Dept. of Archaeology, 1982. 18-20th c. Includes brief pedigrees of those commemorated, with plates of the stones.

Whorlton in Cleveland
HARTLEY, JOAN. 'Stories behind the stones', *J.Cl.F.H.S.* 4(4), 1989, 34-8. Discussion of memorials at Whorlton in Cleveland.

Winestead
Monumental inscriptions, Winestead. E.Y.F.H.S., M.I. **78**. 1994.

Winkersley
See Ripon

Withernsea
Monumental inscriptions, Withernsea. E.Y.F.H.S., M.I. **79**. 1994.

Withernwick
Monumental inscriptions: Withernwick. E.Y.F.H.S., M.I. **24**. 1988.

Woodkirk. Tingley House
MORKHILL, J.W. 'Inscriptions in the burial ground at Tingley House, par. Woodkirk', *Northern genealogist* **2**, 1896, 206-7. Includes will of John Pickering, 1699.

Yeadon
WOLSTENHULME, LES. *Yeadon St. John's memorial inscriptions.* [Leeds]: Wharfedale Family History Group, [1997].
WOLSTENHULME, LES, & CLAYTON, BRIAN. *Wesleyan Methodist Chapel (Chapel Hill), Yeadon: memorial inscriptions in the burial ground, 1827-1935.* Leeds: Wharfedale Family History Group, 1997.

York
BECKERLEGGE, OLIVER A. *Weep not for me: an anthology of poetical epitaphs in York and the surrounding villages.* York: Quack Books, 1985.
BECKERLEGGE, O.A. *Fairwell, vain world: some more poetical epitaphs from York.* Quack Books, 1990.
MORRELL, J.B. *The biography of the common man of the City of York, as recorded in his epitaph.* B.T. Batsford, [1947]. Collection of epitaphs.
MURRAY, HUGH. *The York graveyard guide.* Edinburgh: Saint Andrew Press, 1994. Guide to 32 cemeteries.
ELLISON, PATRICIA M. 'Eighteenth and nineteenth century gravestones: having the last word', in CARVER, MARTIN, ed. *In search of cult: archaeological essays in honour of Philip Rahtz.* Woodbridge: Boydell Press. 1993, 193-202. Brief archaeological study of gravestones at York and Mottram.
STEPHENSON, MILL. 'Monumental brasses in the City of York', *Y.A.J.* **18**, 1904-5, 1-67.

Bar Convent
BELT, A., ed. 'Monumental inscriptions in the cemetery of the Bar Convent, York', *Catholic ancestor* 5(5), 1995, 207-9.

York Minster

BROWNE, JOHN. *Description of the representations and arms on the glass in the windows of York Minster; also the arms on stone,* ed. A.P. Purey-Cust. Leeds: Richard Jackson, 1917.

MORRELL, J.B. *York monuments.* B.T. Batsford, [1944]. Plates of funereal monuments, mainly in York Minster.

PUREY-CUST, A.P. *The heraldry of York Minster: a key to the history of its builders and benefactors, as shewn in the stained-glass windows, and in the carved work in stone.* Leeds: Richard Jackson, 1890. Extensive.

WILLIAMS, J.F. 'The brasses of York Minster', *Transactions of the Monumental Brass Society* 7(8), 1942, 342-52; 8(1), 1944, 1-8.

C. Individual and Family Inscriptions

Armstrong

WILLIAMS, MARY. 'The story behind the stone: a triple tragedy at Marton-in-Cleveland', *J.Cl.F.H.S.* 3(10), 1988, 31-3. Memorial to Robert Armstrong, James Ingledew and Joseph Fenison, 1812.

Armytage

ARMYTAGE, GEORGE J., SIR. 'Stone tablet in Kirby church, Co. York, in memory of Maria Armytage', *M.G.H.* 3rd series **4,** 1902, 280. Includes pedigree, 17-18th c.

'Armytage of Kirklees: inscriptions on the end stones of the niches in the family vault in the chancel of the parish church of Hartshead cum Clifton, in the County of York', *M.G.H.* N.S., **2,** 1877, 116-8. Includes parish register extracts.

Ayrton

WILLIAMS, MARY. 'The story behind the stone: a grave in Coolgardie', *J.Cl.F.H.S.* 3(7), 1987, 39-41. Memorial to William Scrope Ayrton of Cliffden, Saltburn by the Sea, 1898.

Belasyse

See Sotheron

Bower

JEWITT, LLEWELLYN. 'The Bower slab at Bridlington', *Old Yorkshire* **4,** 1883, 166-9. To William Bower, 1671.

Boyle

See Clifford

Boynton

'Roxby and the brass of Thomas Boynton, esquire', *Reliquary* N.S., **7,** 1893, 97-100. 1520.

Brearcy

TURNER, W.B. BARWELL. 'Notes on an armorial window at Adel church', in *Miscellanea* [9]. *T.S.* **28,** 1928, 464-7. Includes the royal arms, and those of Brearcy, Arthington and Kirke.

Briggs

AUTY, ROGER. 'Ferrybridge graveyard', *Cameo* 1993, no. 2, 12-13. Briggs, Hanson and Hutton family inscriptions, 19th c.

Brooke

'Brooke inscriptions: Huddersfield church', *M.G.H.* **1,** 1868, 196-8.

Brus

HODGES, CHARLES C. 'The Brus cenotaph at Guisbrough', *Y.A.J.* **13,** 1895, 226-61. Includes pedigree of Brus of Skelton and Annandale, Dumfriesshire, 11-13th c.

Burlington

See Clifford

Catterick

BROWN, WILLIAM. 'The Catterick brass', *Y.A.J.* **19,** 1906-7, 73-9. Includes folded facsimiles of the brass of Elizabeth Catterick, at Stanwick, 1591.

Cholmley

'Cholmley inscriptions: Whitby', *M.G.H.* **2,** 1876, 222-8.

Clifford

WILTON, RICHARD CECIL. 'The Cliffords and Boyles of Londesborough: with special reference to the Burlington vault in Londesborough church', *T.E.R.A.S.* **14,** 1907, 18-44.

Codd

DALES, S. 'Monuments in St. Mary's Church, Cottingham: the Codd family', *Cottingham Local History Society journal* 6(1), 1982, 225-6. 18-19th c.

Coulthirst

'Monumental brass of Robert Coulthirst at Kirkleatham', *Reliquary* N.S., **6**, 1892, 49-50. 1631.

Coward

WOLSTENHULME, MARGARET. 'Words of wisdom from the tombstone', *Wh.N.* **9**, 1993, 17. Coward memorial at Kellington, 19th c.

Dacre

BOUCH, J. LOWTHER. 'A note on the tombstone of Ranulph, Lord de Dacre of Gillesland in Saxton churchyard, Yorkshire', *Transactions of the Cumberland and Westmorland Antiquarian and Archaeological Society* N.S., **16**, 1916, 229-31. 1461.

FALLOW, T.M. 'The Dacre tomb in Saxton churchyard', *Y.A.J.* **10**, 1889, 303-8.

Dalton

ROUTH, PAULINE E. SHEPPARD. 'A lost brass from Holy Trinity, Goodramgate, York', *Transactions of the Monumental Brass Society* **13**, 1985, 540-42. Dalton family brass, 17th c.

Day

DAVIES, C.R. 'Story behind the stone: under my very nose', *J.Cl.F.H.S.* **5**(12), 1994, 44-7. Memorial to Nancy Day of Bedale, 1832.

Delamotte

INGRAM, M.E. 'The Delamotte family and a monument at Sculcoates', *Y.A.J.* **63**, 1991, 139-52. 18th c.

De La Pole

See Sutton on Hull

De Mauley

MEYRICK, SAMUEL RUSH, SIR. 'Observations on the monumental effigy of De Mauley, formerly in the Minster at York', *Archaeologia* **31**, 1846, 238-48. Includes medieval pedigrees.

Dorman

BURNICLE, ADA. 'Story behind the stone', *J.Cl.F.H.S.* **4**(1), 1989, 28-30. Memorial to Sir Arthur John Dorman, Bt., 1931, at Nunthorpe.

Driver

WILLIAMS, MARY. 'A man with two memorials', *J.Cl.F.H.S.* **3**(4), 1986, 27-8. Memorials to Blaze Driver, 1801.

Dunn

ROUTH, PAULINE SHEPPARD. 'Elegy in a country churchyard', *Church monuments: journal of the Church Monuments Society* **6**, 1991, 47-53. Monument to Thomas Dunn, 1857, at Otley.

Dykes

See Wenslygh

Fenison

See Armstrong

Ferrand

'Brass in Beverley Minster', *Old Yorkshire* **2**, 1881, 62-4. To Richard Ferrand, 1560.

Furness

ALLISON, JOSIE. 'Story behind the stone', *J.Cl.F.H.S.* **3**(12), 1988, 36-8. Memorial of Furness family at Winksley cum Grantley, 18-19th c.

Gascoigne

ROUTH, PAULINE E. SHEPPARD. 'Henry Johnston and the missing lady of Gawthorpe Hall', *Y.A.J.* **54**, 1982, 99-101. Notes on Johnston's sketch of an effigy, believed to be that of Beatrix Gascoigne, 15th c.

Goldesburgh

KAYE, WALTER J. 'Matrix of the brass of John Goldesburgh, 1618, in the Temple Church, London', *Y.A.J.* **32**, 1936, 160-66. 1618.

Grenewood

HOLMES, RICHARD. 'Brass at Darrington near Pontefract', *Y.A.J.* **15**, 1898-99, 214. To James Grenewood of Stapleton, 1670.

Grimsby

HARVEY, A.S. 'A priests tomb at Beverley Minster', *Y.A.J.* **38**, 1951, 504-23. Probably of Gilbert de Grimsby, 1306.

Grisewood

MOON, P.W.H. 'Story behind the stone: an unusual gravestone', *J.Cl.F.H.S.* 5(5), 1993, 41-5. Memorial to John Grisewood of High Worsall, 1729.

Gyles

PEARSON, CHRISTINE. 'A forgotten memorial: the family window of Edmund and Sarah Gyles, and William and Jane Kirby', *York historian* 7, 1986, 34-8. 17th c., from a house in Micklegate Street, York. Includes pedigree of Kirby, 19th c.

Haitfield

MANNING, C.R. 'Notes on a brass of Robert de Haitfield and Ada his wife, Owston church, Yorkshire', *Archaeological journal* 36, 1879, 172-3. 1417.

Hanson

See Briggs

Harland

MENNIM, ELEANOR. *The Harland monuments at All Hallow's church, Sutton on the Forest, York.* [ ]: Croft Press, [1998].

Harrington

'The monumental brass and will of Christopher Harrington, goldsmith, of York, 1614', *Reliquary* N.S. 6, 1892, 211-15. Includes will of Thomas Harrington, 1642.

Hartley

WOLEDGE, HENRY. 'A tombstone noted', *B.T.* 1, 1977, 3. Hartley family, late 19th c.

Hildyard

CAMERON, H.K. 'A palimpsest brass at Winestead, Yorkshire', *Transactions of the Monumental Brass Society* 11, 1975, 386-95. Hildyard family brass, 11th c.

Hopton

See Metcalfe

Howgego

SAMPSON, ALEX. 'Story behind the stone', *J.Cl.F.H.S.* 4(8), 1990, 28-30. Memorial to William J.Howgego of Whitby, 1901.

Hutton

See Briggs

Ingledew

See Armstrong

Lamplough

FENTON, R.V. 'The mystery of Lamplough family memorials in Langtoft church', *East Yorkshire Local History Society bulletin* 55, 1996/7, 16-17.

Langton

BADHAM, SALLY. 'A lost bronze effigy of 1279 from York Minster', *Antiquaries journal* 60, 1980, 59-65. Commemorating Dean William de Langton, 1279.

Lascelles

LANKESTER, PHILIP J. 'Two lost effigial monuments in Yorkshire and the evidence of church notes', *Church monuments: journal of the Church Monuments Society* 8, 1993, 25-44. Of Lascelles at Escrick, and (probably) Lound at South Cave.

Markenfield

PLANCHE, J.R. 'On an effigy of one of the Markenfield family in Ripon Cathedral', *Journal of the British Archaeological Association* 20, 1864, 285-96. Sir Thomas Markenfield, 14th c. Includes genealogical notes.

Metcalfe

SAYWELL, J.L. 'Two Yorkshire monumental slabs', *Y.G.* 1, 1888, 230-33. To Rev. Mark Metcalfe, 1593, and Sir Roger Hopton, 1506.

Metham

See Saltmarshe

Miles

KIRBY, RICHARD. 'The story behind the stone', *J.Cl.F.H.S.* 3(6), 1987, 34-6. Memorial to William Miles of Bridlington, 1884.

Mudd

WINSPUR, A. 'Story behind the stone: where is the gravestone?' *J.Cl.F.H.S.* 3(9), 1988, 24-7. Memorial to Matthew Marsden Mudd of Crakehall, undated.

Myers

WOLSTENHULME, LES. 'A mining tragedy', *Wh.N.* **14**, 1994, 12-13. Memorial to James Myers of Yeadon, 1848.

Paget

SHARPE, ALLISON E. 'The Paget memorial, St. Mary's, Skirpenbeck: some problems considered', *Y.A.J.* **65**, 1993, 95- 114. 17th c.

SHARPE, ALLISON E. 'A Paget memorial in perspective: aspects of a seventeenth-century funerary monument erected to Richard Paget in St. Mary's, Skirpenbeck, East Riding of Yorkshire', *Antiquaries journal* **70**, 1990, 65-81. 1636.

Percy

GOLDBERG, P.J.P. 'The Percy tomb in Beverley Minster', *Y.A.J.* **56**, 1984, 65-74. 14th c.

Price

See Sotheron

Pudsay

BUTLER, LAWRENCE. 'A lost brass inscriptions from Stanwick church', *Y.A.J.* **59**, 1987, 185-6. To Edina Pudsay, 1485.

Redman

KNOWLES, RICHARD. 'Re-identification of a Harewood alabaster', *Wakefield Historical Society journal* **2**, 1975, 34-9. Memorial of Edward Redman, 1510; includes facsimile of will, and Redman pedigree, 15-16th c.

Richardson

STEPHENSON, MILL. 'A brass recently replaced in Knaresborough church', *Y.A.J.* **21**, 1910-11, 484. Of Thomas Richardson, 1683.

'Monumental inscriptions of Bradford worthies', *B.A.* N.S., **3**, 1912, 95-6. Memorials of John Richardson, 1735, and Joseph Thwaites, 1799.

Rockingham

WRAGG, R.B. 'The Rockingham mausoleum (1784-1793)', *Y.A.J.* **52**, 1980, 157-66.

WRAGG, R.B. 'Four monuments at Wentworth', *Transactions of the Ancient Monuments Society* N.S. **23**, 1978, 29-39. Rockingham family memorials.

St. Quinton

STEPHENSON, MILL. 'An incised alabaster slab in Harpham church', *T.E.R.A.S.* **10**, 1903, 25-6. To Sir William de St. Quinton, 1349.

Saltmarshe

BADHAM, SALLY, GITTOS, BRIAN, & GITTOS, MOIRA. 'The fourteenth-century monuments in the Saltmarshe Chapel at Howden, Yorkshire: their history and context', *Y.A.J.* **68**, 1996, 113-55. Saltmarshe and Metham family memorials.

Salvin

SPENCER, W.M. 'A brass inscription from Lowthorpe, near Driffield', *Y.A.J.* **59**, 1987, 183-4. To George Salvin, 1416.

Sandford

WILLIAMS, MARY. 'The story behind the stone: grave of a hero', *J.Cl.F.H.S.* **3**(8), 1987, 28-30. Memorial to Dick Sandford of Exmouth, Devon, at Eston.

Scrope

FRENCH, T.W. 'The tomb of Archbishop Scrope in York Minster', *Y.A.J.* **61**, 1989, 95-102. 1405.

Selley

WALTER, D. ALLEYNE. 'Monumental slab, Gorhill church, East Yorks', *Reliquary* N.S., **3**, 1889, 193-4. Monumental inscription to Joan Selley, c.15th c.

Slingsby

ATKINSON, W.A. 'William Slingsby and the Slingsby monuments in Knaresborough church', *Y.A.J.* **36**, 1944-7, 366-73.

WHITE, ADAM. 'Thomas Browne, William Wright, and the Slingsby monument at Knaresborough', *Y.A.J.* **69**, 1997, 193-208, 17th c.

Smyth

CHATTEN, JANICE. 'Unusual monument to Charles Piazzi Smyth', *R.H.* **3**(12), 1998, 319. 1900, at Sharow.

Sotheron

SOTHERON, CHARLES. 'Sotheron, Thompson and Price monumental inscriptions', *M.G.H.* N.S., **1**, 1874, 302-14. Mainly in Yorkshire and Middlesex; includes notes on Belasyse of Henknoll and Newburgh.

Stockdale

THOMAS, A.B. 'Story behind the stone: Prince Stockdale, 1817-1884', *J.Cl.F.H.S.* 5(9), 1994, 40-42. Of Stainton.

Sutton on Hull

HARVEY, A.S. 'Notes on two heraldic tombs', *Y.A.J.* 40, 1962, 462-77. Tombs of Sir John Sutton, of Sutton, and Sir William De La Pole of Hull, mid-14th c.
'[Brass rubbing]', *R.H.* 1(10), 1992, 4-5. Memorial of Thomas Sutton, late 15th c.

Talbot

H., M.F. 'The Talbot tombs', *N. & Q.* 1(1), 1899, 1-2. In Sheffield.

STACYE, JOHN. 'On the monuments in the Shrewsbury Chapel in parish church, Sheffield', *Journal of the British Archaeological Association* 30, 1874, 175-81. Talbot family memorials.

Teyll

COLLIER, C.V. 'An unrecorded East Riding brass at Harpham', *T.E.R.A.S.* 10, 1903, 70. Includes rubbing of brass to Thomas Teyll, 1581.

Thompson

'Monumental inscriptions to members of the Thompson family', *Cottingham Local History Society journal* 11(1) 1989, 28-9. Early 19th c.
See also Sotheron

Thoresby

LUMB, G.D. 'John Thoresby', in *Miscellanea* [6]. *T.S.* 22, 1915, 55-7. Monumental inscription, 1679.

Thwaites

ROUTH, PAULINE SHEPPARD. 'The Thwaites family and their effigies at Lund, East Riding', *Y.A.J.* 61, 1989, 85-94. 15-16th c.
See also Richardson

Topcliffe

WHITING, CHARLES EDWIN. 'The Topcliffe brass', *Transactions of the Monumental Brass Society* 7(1), 1934, 23-7. Commemorating Thomas of Topcliffe and his wife Mabel, 1391.

Towneley

'The Towneley brass, York', *Old Yorkshire* 2, 1881, 68-9. Extract from *Palatine notebook*. 1712.

Turner

TAYLOR, A.C. 'Kirkleatham', *Architectural review* 124, 1958, 247-50. Mausoleum commemorating Marwood William Turner, 1740.
'Inscription on a brass tablet in St. Hilda's church, Whitby', *B.A.* N.S. 2, 1905, 245. Memorial of John Turner, 1884.

Ward

'Ward', *Y.G.* 1, 1888, 168-9. Monumental inscriptions of the Ward family of Whitby, in Wandsworth church, 18th c.

Washington

TURNER, W.B. BARWELL. 'The Washington shield at Selby Abbey', in *Miscellanea* [9]. *T.S.* 29, 1928, 181-93.

Welles

ROUTH, PAULINE SHEPPARD. 'Lionel, Lord Welles, and his Methley monument', *Y.A.J.* 63, 1991, 77-83. 1461.

Wenslygh

RAINE, JAMES. 'Notes of a remarkable sepulchral brass of Flemish design, in the church of Wensley, Yorkshire', *Archaeological journal* 12, 1855, 238-43. Memorials to Simon de Wenslygh, 14th c., and Oswald Dykes, 1607.

Wharton

'Monuments of Thomas Lord Wharton', *Herald and genealogist* 1, 1863, 182-5. At Healaugh, 1568.

3. PROBATE RECORDS

A. *General*

Wills are invaluable sources of genealogical information, usually giving the names of the testator's surviving children, and sometimes much more. For a brief general guide to the location of Yorkshire wills, see:

CHAPPLE, CHRISTINE E. 'Wills: the flesh on the bones. A brief guide on how to locate wills in Yorkshire', *Y.F.H.* 13(5), 1987, 99-101; 13(6), 1987, 124-5.

The various probate jurisdictions in Yorkshire are listed in:

LAWTON, GEORGE. *A brief treatise of Bona Notabilia, together with an account of the Archiepiscopal courts of probate within the Province of York, and of the other courts of probate in the counties of York and Nottingham, and an alphabetical list of such parishes and chapelries within the said counties as are not under the ordinary jurisdiction of the Archbishop of York in matters of probate and administration.* J. Butterworth & Son, 1825. Written for legal practitioners.

Until 1858, wills were mainly proved in ecclesiastical courts, although a few manorial courts also had probate jurisdiction. The county was in the Province of York; the major probate court was the Prerogative Court of York. Wills proved in this court are indexed in a number of Yorkshire Archaeological Society Record Series volumes:

Index of wills in the York Registry, 1389 to [1602]. 6 vols. Y.A.S., R.S. 6, 11, 14, 19, 22 & 24, 28, 32. 1889-98. Also includes administration acts. Contents: v.6. 1389 to 1514; v.11. 1514 to 1553; v.14. 1554 to 1568, ed. A Gibbons; v.19. 1568 to 1585; v.22. 1585 to 1594; v.24. 1594 to 1602; v.26. 1603 to 1611; v.28. 1612 to 1619; v.32. 1620 to 1627; v.35. 1626 to 1636 (administrations 1627-1652).

COLLINS, F., ed. *Wills in the York Registry from 1636 to 1652.* Y.A.S., R.S. 4. 1888.

CROSSLEY, E.W., ed. *Index of wills, administrations, and probate acts in the York Registry, A.D.1660 to 1665, and also of the unregistered wills and the probate acts, Aug.1, 1633 to July 31, 1634, and of the 're infecta' wills and the wills in bundles A and B.* Y.A.S., R.S. 49. 1913.

CROSSLEY, E.W., ed. *Index of wills, administrations and probate acts in the Yorks. Registry, A.D.1666 to 1672, and also of the wills etc. in certain peculiars.* Y.A.S., R.S. 60. 1920. The peculiar courts whose wills are indexed include those of Aldborough (manorial) 1610-1700, Beverley, 1539-52, Hexham, 1593-1602, the Dean and Chapter of York, 1336-43 and 1352-1429, and St. Leonards Hospital, York.

CROSSLEY, E.W., ed. *Index of wills, administrations and probate acts in the York Registry, A.D.1673 to 1680 and also of wills etc. in the Peculiar of Beeford, together with tables of all printed indexes and of the principal collections of abstracts of Yorkshire wills, etc.* Y.A.S., R.S. 68. 1926. For 1586-1768.

CROSSLEY, E.W., ed. *Index of wills, administrations, and probate acts in the York Registry, A.D. 1681 to A.D.1688, including the 'vacancies' June to August 1683 and April 1686 to December 1688.* Y.A.S., R.S. 89. 1934. In the Exchequer and Prerogative courts, and the Dean and Chapter's, during the vacancy of the see.

Briefer indexes, mainly covering Northumberland and Co.Durham, but also including some Yorkshire wills, are printed in:

'Index of wills, admons., etc., at the Prerogative Court of York, 1827-34', *J.Cl.F.H.S.* 2(2), 1982, 13-16, & 18-19.

'Index of wills, admons, etc., at the Prerogative Court of York, 1835-42', *J.Cl.F.H.S.* 27(3), 1983, 15-18; 2(5), 1983, 11-13.

Many wills from the Prerogative Court of York have been abstracted in a series of Surtees Society volumes:

RAINE, JAMES, ed. *Testamenta Eboracensia, or, wills registered at York illustrative of the history, manners, language, and statistics, &c., of the Province of York from the year MCCC downwards. Part 1.* Surtees Society 4. 1836. Selected transcripts, 1316-1430.

[RAINE, JAMES, junior], ed. *Testamenta Eboracensia: a selection of wills from the registry at York, part II.* Surtees Society 30. 1855. Selection, 1429-67, with index to pt.1 included.

[RAINE, JAMES, junior], ed. *Testamenta Eboracensia: a selection of wills from the registry at York, vol.III.* Surtees Society, **45**. 1865. Mainly 15th c., includes 'dispensations for marriage, marriage licences, etc., from the registers of the Archbishops, the bishops of Durham, and the Archdeacons of Richmond, 1374-1531.

Testamenta Eboracensia: a selection of wills from the Registry at York, vol. IV. Surtees Society, **53**. 1869. For 1420-1509. Includes further 'dispensations for marriage, marriage licences, etc'.

Testamenta Eboracensia: a selection of wills from the Registry at York, vol V. Surtees Society **79**. 1884. Covers 1509-31.

CLAY, JOHN WM. ed. *Testamenta Eboracensia: a selection of wills from the registry at York, vol.VI.* Surtees Society **106**. 1902. 1516-50.

See also:

HUNTER, JOSEPH. 'A few notes on manuscripts, from wills in the register at York', in *Memoirs illustrative of the history and antiquities of the County and City of York communicated to the annual meeting of the Archaeological Institute of Great Britain and Ireland, held at York, July 1846 ...* John Murray, 1847, 10-24. Bequests of manuscripts identified in wills.

Wills from the Consistory Court of the Archbishop of York are indexed in:

CROSSLEY, E.W. *Index of the original documents of the Consistory Court of York, A.D.1427 to A.D.1658, and also of the probate and administration acts in the court of the Dean of York, A.D.1604 to A.D.1722.* Y.A.S., R.S. **73**. 1928. The 'original documents' of the title are probate records.

For wills entered in the Archbishops' registers, see:

Index of the wills and administrations entered in the registers of the Archbishops at York, being Consistory wills, &c., A.D.1316 to A.D.1822, known as the Archbishops wills. Y.A.S., R.S. **93**. 1937. This is continued by:

'Chancery court probate index, 1825-1857', *B.I.B.* **1**, 1975-8, 39-42.

For wills of the York Dean and Chapter, see: *Index of wills, etc., from the Dean and Chapter's court at York, A.D.1321 to 1636, with appendix of original wills A.D.1524 to 1724.* Y.A.S., R.S. **38**. 1907.

See also:

'An index of York probate material &c', *Family history* **1**(2), 1962, 38-41. Index to Deanery act books. Continued by:

'Wills and admons. etc., listings taken from Cals. of old Diocese of York and Diocese of Lincoln', *Family history* **2**(7), 1963, 7-8; 2(9), 1964, 90-92; 2(10), 1964, 103-5; 3(13), 1965, 29-32.

The Prerogative Court of Canterbury was the premier court of probate in England and a few wills relating to Yorkshire were proved there. Indexes to the records of this court covering the whole country are listed in my *English genealogy: a bibliography,* to which you should refer.

During the Interregnum, all Yorkshire wills were proved in the Prerogative Court of Canterbury; these are indexed in:

COLLINS, FRANCIS, ed. *A catalogue of the Yorkshire wills at Somerset House, for the years 1649 to 1660.* Y.A.S., R.S. **1**. 1885, 49-296.

Abstracts of many of these wills are printed in:

CLAY, JOHN WILLIAM. *Abstracts of Yorkshire wills in the time of the Commonwealth at Somerset House, London, chiefly illustrative of Sir John William Dugdale's visitation of Yorkshire in 1665-6.* Y.A.S., R.S. **9**. 1890.

Abstracts of earlier Yorkshire wills proved in the Prerogative Court of Canterbury (and in the Court of Arches) are printed in:

CLAY, JOHN WM., ed. *North country wills, being abstracts of wills relating to the counties of York, Nottingham, Northumberland, Cumberland and Westmorland, at Somerset House and Lambeth Palace, 1383 to 1558.* Surtees Society **116**. 1908.

CLAY, JOHN WM., ed. *North country wills, being abstracts of wills relating to the counties of York, Nottingham, Northumberland, Cumberland and Westmorland, 1558-1604.* Surtees Society **121**. 1912.

For 14-15th c. Yorkshire wills at Lambeth Palace, see:
SMITH, J. CHALLENOR. 'Wills deposited at Lambeth', *Y.A.J.* **24**, 1917, 103-4. Brief list, 14-15th c.
Forty-four miscellaneous probate inventories held by the Yorkshire Archaeological Society are edited in:
BREARS, PETER C.D., ed. *Yorkshire probate inventories, 1542-1689.* Y.A.S., R.S. **134**. 1972.

B. Local Collections

A wide variety of other local courts exercised probate jurisdiction in the county. Manorial courts which had probate jurisdiction are listed in:
LAWTON, GEORGE. 'Manorial courts in the counties of York and Nottingham which exercise the right of proving wills and granting letters of administration', *Family history* 5(28/9); N.S. **4-5**, 1968, 154-9. List; originally published 1829.
A number of collections and indexes of probate records covering particular localities have been published; these are listed here.

Abbotside
THWAITE, HARTLEY, ed. *Abstracts of Abbotside wills 1552-1688.* Y.A.S., R.S., **130**. 1968.

Aldbrough
'Aldbrough manor court (West Riding)', *Northern genealogist* **4**, 1901, 65. List of wills, 17th c.

Altofts
'Manor court of Altofts in Normanton, Co.York: wills and administration', *Northern genealogist* **1**, 1895, 130.

Arkengarthdale
'Manor court of Arkengarthdale: original wills', *Northern genealogist* **4**, 1901, 93-102 & 116-31; **5**, 1902, 24-9; **6**, 1903, 93-6. Incomplete; reached 'Milner' when the *Northern genealogist* ceased publication.

Attercliffe
SHAW, A.B. 'Ancient Attercliffe wills (1550-1700)', *T.Hunter A. S.* **2**(2), 1921, 165-75. Discussion.

Barnoldswick
KIRK, G.E., ed. 'Some documents of Barnoldswick manor court of probate' in WHITING, C.E., ed. *Miscellanea* **6**. Y.A.S., R.S., **118**. 1953, 53-84. For 1660-1794; mainly probate inventories.

Barwick in Elmet
LUMB, GEORGE DENISON *Wills, registers and monumental inscriptions of the parish of Barwick in Elmet, co.York.* Leeds: Privately printed, 1908. Includes wills proved in the York Exchequer and Prerogative courts to 1750, plus a few from the Prerogative Court of Canterbury, also parish registers 1653-1812, and monumental inscriptions.

Batley
See Westerdale

Bedale
BUMSTEAD, K.M. 'Wills and inventories in the Bedale area of North Yorkshire', *Y.A.J.* **57**, 1985, 163-76. General discussions, 1539-1720.

Bingley
See Crosley

Bradford
'Translation of the earliest local wills in the York registry', *B.A.* **1**, 1888, 201-3; **2**, 1895, 19-22, 169-72, 218-20 & 247-50.

Cottingley
See Crosley

Craven
STOTT, BRIAN. *Index to Craven wills proved at York, Jan. 1800-Oct 1830, covering the ecclesiastical parishes of Barnoldswick, Bolton by Bowland, Bracewell, Gisburn, Long Preston, Mitton, Slaidburn, plus numerous entries of Lancashire wills proved at York.* 1 fiche. [ ]: Lancashire Family History and Heraldry Society, [198-?]
Index to West Craven and Lancashire wills proved at York Sep. 1853-Feb.1858 **W7**. 1 fiche. [ ]: Lancashire Family History and Heraldry [198-?] Covers Barnoldswick, Bolton by Bowland, Bracewell, Gisburn, Long Preston, Mitton and Slaidburn.

Crosley

PRESTON, WILLIAM E., ed. *Wills proved in the court of the manor of Crosley, Bingley, Cottingley and Pudsey, in Co. York, with inventories and abstracts of bonds.* 3 pts. Local record series **1**. Bradford: Bradford Historical and Antiquarian Society, 1914-29. Early 17th c. transcripts.

Doncaster

HEY, DAVID G., ed. *Doncaster people of ten generations ago.* Sheffield: University of Sheffield Dept. of Extramural Studies / Workers Educational Association, Yorkshire District (South), 1975. Abstracts of 23 probate inventories, 1694-1726.

Feliskirk

BROWN, WILLIAM. 'Extracts from wills relating to the church', *Y.A.S.* **22**, 1913, 203-5. Of Feliskirk, 15-16th.

Halifax

KENDALL, H.P. 'Gleanings from local Elizabethan wills', *P.R.H.A.S.* 1915, 113-48. General discussion of bequests.

CLAY, J.W., & CROSSLEY, E.W., eds. *Halifax wills, being abstracts and translations of the wills registered at York from the parish of Halifax.* 2 vols. [ ]: Privately printed, [1906]. [v.1.] Part I. 1389 to 1514, ed. J.W.Clay. Part II. 1515 to 1544 ... ed. E.W. Crossley. v.II. 1545-1559, ed. E.W.Crossley.

Haworth

'A history of Haworth, part one', *K.D.F.H.S.J.* Spring 1996, 22-5. Extracts from Haworth wills, 16-17th c.

Holderness

BROWN, WILLIAM. 'Holderness wills extracted from the Probate Registry at York, *T.E.R.A.S.* **10**, 1903, 1-18; **11**, 1903, 1-18. Medieval; in Latin.

Horbury

BARTLETT, K.S., ed. *The will of Horbury 1404-1688.* Wakefield: Wakefield Metropolitan District Council, 1979. Continued in two volumes for 1688-1757 (1980) and 1757-1809 (1981).

Hull

BOYLE, J.B. 'Wills enrolled in the *Liber Rubeus* of Kingston-upon-Hull', *Northern genealogist* **2**, 1896, 181-3.

Kirkby Malzeard

See Masham

Knaresborough

[COLLINS, FRANCIS], ed. *Wills & administrations from the Knaresborough court rolls.* 2 vols. Surtees Society **104** & **110**. 1902-5. Contents: v.1. 1516-51. v.2. 1607-68; also 'index to original wills, &c., at Somerset House proved at Knaresborough 1640 to 1858'.

Leeds

BRIGG, WILLIAM, ed. 'Testamenta Leodiensia, extracted from the Probate Registry at York', in *Miscellanea* 1. *T.S.* **2**, 1891, 99-110 & 205-14; *Miscellanea 2. T.S.* **4**, 1895, 1-16 & 139-47; *Miscellanea* [3]. *T.S.* **9**, 1899, 81-96, 160-92 & 246-77; *Miscellanea* [4] *T.S.* **11**, 1904, 37-68; *Miscellanea* [5]. *T.S.* **15**, 1909, 10-25, Leeds wills, 14-16th c.

COOK, ROBERT BEILBY. 'Wills of Leeds and district', in *Miscellanea* [6]. *T.S.* **22**, 1915, 85-102 & 235-64; *Miscellanea* [7]. *T.S.* **24**, 1919, 39-66 & 304-35; *Miscellanea* [8]. *T.S.* **26**, 1924, 172-220 & 311-49. Medieval.

LUMB, GEORGE DENISON. ed. *Testamenta Leodiensia: wills of Leeds, Pontefract, Wakefield, Otley and district, 1539 to 1553. T.S.* **19**. 1913.

LUMB, GEORGE DENISON, ed. *Wills of Leeds, Pontefract, Wakefield, Otley and district, 1553 to 1561. T.S.* **27**. 1930.

Masham

Masham peculier court: an indexed calendar of wills and administrations. 2 pts. Ripon: Ripon Historical Society/Ripon, Harrogate & District Family History Group, 1994. Pt. 1. The calendar. Pt. 2. The indexes. The peculiar covered Masham and Kirkby Malzeard parishes; this is an index to the innumerable wills proved in this court.

'Peculiar court of Masham: a collection of the indexes at Somerset House and at York Probate Registry from the commencement down to 1709', *Northern genealogist* **4,** 1901, 132-6; **5,** 1902, 30-32, 103-5 & 153-6; **6,** 1903, 16-22 & 86-9. Incomplete; alphabetical arrangement to 'Rownthwaite' only.

Pontefract
See Leeds

Pudsey
See Crosley

Otley
See Leeds

Richmond Archdeaconry
RAINE, JAMES, junior, ed. *Wills and inventories from the registry of the Archdeaconry of Richmond, extending over portions of the counties of York, Westmorland, Cumberland and Lancashire.* Surtees Society **26.** 1853. Mainly 16th c.
'Richmondshire wills (Eastern deaneries), being a calendar to the probate records formerly in the custody of the Archdeacon of Richmond', *Northern genealogist* **2,** 1896, supplement. Incomplete; to Gristhwaite only.
'Some wills from the Richmond registry', *Northern genealogist* **3,** 1900, 25-8, 109-12, & 124-30; **4,** 1901, 41-8. Abstracts.

Rothwell
COOK, ROBERT BEILBY, ed. 'Wills of the parishes of Rothwell, Saxton, Sherburn in Elmet, Swillington, Thorner, Whitkirk and Woodkirk,' in *Miscellanea. T.S.* **33,** 1935, 22-60.

Saxton
See Rothwell

Selby
COLLINS, F., ed. *Selby wills.* Y.A.S., R.S. **47.** 1912. For 1634-1710; also includes marriage licences and bonds, 1664-1726.

Sheffield
'Index to wills, admons., etc., at the Prerogative Court of York' *F.S.* **4**(3), 1983, 58-60; **4**(4), 1983, 83-4. For the Sheffield area. Incomplete; A-G only.
'Sheffield wills proved at York, 1400 to 1600', in HALL, T. WALTER. *Yorkshire historical sketches.* Sheffield: J.W.Northend, 1931, 117-26. List.

Sherburn in Elmet
See Rothwell

South Cave
KANER, JENNIFER, et al, eds. *Goods and chattels, 1552-1642: wills, farm and household inventories from the parish of South Cave in the East Riding of Yorkshire.* Hull: University of Hull Centre for Continuing Education, Development and Training, 1994.

Startforth
'Startforth wills', *T.R.S.* **5,** 1939-40, 6-8. List 1611-1826.

Swillington
See Rothwell

Temple Newsam
KIRK, G.E. 'Wills, inventories and bonds of the manor courts of Temple Newsam, W.R.Yorks., 1612-1701', in *Miscellanea* **[10]**. *T.S.* **33,** 1935, 241-82. 130 transcripts.

Thirsk
BROWN, WILLIAM. 'Extracts from wills relating to the church', *Y.A.J.* **22,** 1913, 216-25. Of Thirsk, 15-16th c.

Thorner
See Rothwell

Wakefield
'Wills &c., in the peculiar courts at Wakefield', *Northern genealogist* **1,** 1895, 33-7 & 110-12; **2,** 1896, 102-7 & 168-71. 17-19th c.
See also Leeds

Warmfield
'Manor court of Warmfield with Heath, Co. York: wills and administrations', *Northern genealogist* **1,** 1895, 129. List.

Westerdale

CROSSLEY, E.W., ed. 'The testamentary documents of Yorkshire peculiars', in *Miscellanea* 2. Y.A.S., R.S. **74**, 1929, 46-86. Includes abstracts of wills from Westerdale and Batley, with lists of other probate records for these two peculiars.

Whitby

VICKERS, N. *A Yorkshire town in the eighteenth century: the probate inventories of Whitby, North Yorkshire, 1700-1800*. Studley: K.A.F. Brewin Books, 1986.

Whitkirk

See Rothwell

Woodkirk

See Rothwell

York

COOK, R. BEILBY. 'Some early civic wills of York', *Reports and papers of the Associated Architectural Societies* **28**(2), 1906, 827-71; **31**(1), 1911, 319-39; **32**(1), 1913, 293-317; **32**(2), 1914, 569-93; **33**(1), 1915, 161-77; **33**(2), 1916, 473-92; **34**(1), 1917, 201-17; **35**(1), 1919, 61-74. Medieval.

CROSS, CLAIRE, ed. *York clergy wills, 1520-1600*. B.T.C. **10** & **15**. York: Bk.I.H.R., 1984-89. v.1. Minster clergy. v.2. City clergy. Full abstracts.

C. *Individual and Family Wills*

Many probate records relating to particular individuals have been published in journals; these are listed here. Many others included in works of wider interest are mentioned elsewhere in this bibliography.

Almack

'Original documents', *Archaeological journal* **5**, 1848, 316-21. Includes wills of John and Richard Almack of Sandhutton, 1558.

Appleby

'Will of Peter Appleby', *T.R.S.* **14**, 1945, 6. Of Barforth, 1605.

Atkinson

'The will of William Atkinson', *B.T.* **13**, 1982, 26. Of Patrington, 1697.

Barker

CROSS, CLAIRE. 'A medieval Yorkshire library', *N.H.* **25**, 1989, 281-90. Based on the will and probate inventory of Robert Barker, vicar of Driffield.

Barras

'The will of Thomas Barras of Upper Green, West Ardsley', *Cameo* 1994, no.1, 9-13. 1745.

Beal

See Dawson

Bean

'Bean of Jamaica', *Northern genealogist* **1**, 1895, 131-2. Will of James Bean of Jamaica and Aldbrough, 1766.

Benson

'Benson notes', *Y.C.M.* **2**, 1892, 222-31. Extracts from wills.

Berry

See Levet

Braithwaite

'Unpublished wills (7)', *R.H.* **2**(6), 1994, 122. Will of John Braithwaite of Ripon, gent, 1680

Branwell

'Aunt Branwell's will', *B.I.B.* **47**(1), 1987, 17-18. Will of Elizabeth Branwell, 1833 (proved 1842).

Bright

'The will of Timothy Bright, M.D., rector of Methley and Barwick-in-Elmet', *Y.A.J.* **17**, 1902-3, 50-54. 1615. Includes pedigree.

Brooksbank

'Will of John Brooksbank of Bradford', *B.A.* **9**; N.S. **7**, 1952, 256. 1756 (proved 1759)

Browne

'Unpublished wills (3)', *R.H.* **2**(2), 1993, 27. Will of John Browne, 1597.

Bubwith

'The will of Nicholas Bubwith, Bishop of Bath and Wells', *Y.C.M.* **2**, 1892, 220-22. 1424.

Burton

'Unpublised wills (5)', *R.H.* 2(4), 1993, 81. Will of Daniel Burton of Ripon, 1682.

WHITEHEAD, J.R. 'The will of Robert Burton jnr., 1667', *Cottingham Local History Society journal* 3(1), 1964, 5-6.

WHITEHOUSE, J.R. 'Richard Burton's will, 1635', *Cottingham Local History Society journal* 1(25), 1956, 83.

Capper

DRURY, CHARLES. 'Will of Christopher Capper, 1636', *T.Hunter A.S.* 3, 1929, 24-33. Includes pedigrees of Capper, Barbour and Sanderson, 17th c.

Cockcroft

GLEDHILL, BARBER. 'Cockrofts of Mayroyd', *T.Hal.A.S.* 1962, 45-59. 17-18th c. wills; also includes abstract of deed of partition, 1774.

Constable

SPEDDING, CARLISLE J.S., ed. 'Documents at Everingham, the property of Lord Herries', in *Miscellanea* 4. C.R.S. 4. 1907, 267-71. Includes will of Sir Philip Constable, Bt., 1664.

Conyers

KNOWLES, RICHARD. 'A 16th century funeral account', *Wakefield Historical Society journal* 6, 1979, 1-16. Of John, 3rd Lord Conyers, 1557.

Cooper

'Sir Edmund Cooper, royalist and mayor of York', *Northern genealogist* 1, 1896, 65-6. Includes will, 1670, and monumental inscription.

Cowton

'The will of John Cowton of Scarborough, goldsmith, 1558', *Reliquary* N.S., 8, 1894, 178-9.

Cromwell

HERSEY, C. 'Cromwell wills', *M.G.H.* 3rd series 1, 1896, 47 & 95. Of Nottinghamshire and Yorkshire, 15-16th c.

Crosby

WOOLRICH, GILL. 'Where there's a will ...', *C.Y.D.F.H.S.J.* 27, 1992, 26-7. Extracts from will of Stephen Crosby of Robin Hood's Bay 1839.

Dallariver

S., J. 'Curious will', *Y.C.M.* 1, 1891, 156-7. Of Thomas Dallariver of Helmsley, 1597.

Dawson

CURRY, JANE. 'The humble admon.', *Y.F.H.* 15(2), 1989, 44. Note on administration bonds for Richard Dawson 1738, and Ann Beal, 1853.

'Unpublished wills (8)', *R.H.* 2(6), 1994, 122. Will of Thomas Dawson of Bondgate, Ripon, 1681.

Denbigh

MORRIS, COLIN DENBIGH 'How to become a valuable ancestor', *Bod-kin* 26, 1992, 10-11. Discussion of the will of Mary Denbigh of Headingley, 1866.

Fairbanks

WHITING, CAROLINE 'Will of George Fairbanks, of Yorkshire, England', *New England historical & genealogical register* 7, 1853, 303-4. Of Somerby, Halifax, 1650.

Firth

'A physicians household goods in 1769', *B.A.* 8; N.S., 6, 1940, 25-8. Probate inventory of Joshua Firth.

Foster

BARNARD, JOHN, & BELL, MAUREEN. *The early seventeenth-century York book trade and John Foster's inventory of 1616.* Leeds: Leeds Philosophical and Literary Society, 1994. Includes wills of Anthony Foster, 1610, and Margaret Foster, 1613, with biographical notes on 'John Foster's appraisers and debtors', with extracts from his probate inventory.

Fysh

FYSH, J.P.G., & FYSH, A.V.G.A. 'A 17th century clergyman's worldly possessions', *Y.F.H.* 13(3), 1987, 65-6. Based on the will and inventory of Rev. Phatuel Fysh, 1677, rector of Staveley.

Gargrave

CARTWRIGHT, J.J. Inventory of the goods of Sir Cotton Gargrave of Nostell in 1588', *Y.A.J.* 11, 1891, 279-86.

'Gargrave of Nostell', *Northern genealogist* 1, 1895, 137-8. Will of Sir Cotton Gargrave, 1585.

Greenwood

KENDALL, HUGH P. 'Hollinhey in Sowerby', *P.R.H.A.S.* 1920, 1-27. Includes will and inventory of John Greenwood of Hollinhey, 1643.

Hamerton

'Hamerton family', *Y.G.* 1, 1888, 84-6. List of wills, 1383-1787.

Hanson

'[Hanson family wills, 18-19th c.]', *K.D.F.H.S.J.* Winter 1996, 8-10.

Harrison

SIMPSON, JUSTIN. 'Harrison of Sedburgh and Stamford', *Northern genealogist* 1, 1895, 165-6. Will of Reginald Harrison, 1594.

SIMPSON, JUSTIN. 'Harrysons of Sedbergh', *Y.G.* 2, 1890, 102-5. Will of Reginald Harrison, 1597.

Harsnett

MUSKETT, J.J. 'Archbishop Harsnett and his will', *East Anglian* N.S., 12, 1907-8, 293-6. 1631.

Hartley

STEPHEN, ROSEMARY, ed. 'Hartley, of Suffolk & Lancs', *Suffolk roots: the journal of the Suffolk Genealogy Society* 10(4), 1984, 77. Will of Robert Hartley of Thornton in Craven, 1607.

Hexham

'Ecclesiastical Middlesborough in medieval times', *Y.A.J.* 18, 1904-5, 68-73. Mainly notes on wills; includes transcript of will of John Hexham, 1554/5.

Hooke

CROSSLEY, E.W. 'Two Halifax vicars: the wills and inventories of Richard Hooke and Edmund Hough', *P.R.H.A.S.* 1904-5, 113-27. 1688 and 1690.

Hoppay

'Hoppay wills', *Y.N.Q.* 3, 1893, 110-11. Will of Edward Hoppay of Wakefield, 1548.

Horsfall

'Horsfall wills', *Y.C.M.* 1, 1891, 327-9. 18th c., includes will of John Horsfall of Underbank, 1711/12, and various deeds.

Hough

See Hooke

Hudson

HUDSON, D. 'The will of William Hudson, *Cameo* 1995, no.2, 7. Of Drighlington, 1863.

HUDSON, D. 'Extracts from will of William Hudson, Drighlington', *Bod-kin* 11, 1988, 3. Will dated 1863, proved 1864.

Ingilby

See Middleton

Jackson

SNELL, BEATRICE S. 'Martha Jackson's minority: Yorkshire trustees accounts, 1722-1728', *Journal of the Friends Historical Society* 45(1), 1953, 6-14.

Kendall

'Kendall family', *Y.C.M.* 2, 1892, 27-31. Wills, 16-18th c.

Langstaffe

'Will of William Langstaffe of Romaldkirke, Co. York, 1627', *M.G.H.* N.S., 4, 1884, 115.

Lawe

'The will of Richard Lawe of Halifax, goldsmith, 1565', *Reliquary* N.S., 8, 1894, 179.

Layton

CUDWORTH, WM. 'The Layton family of Rawdon', *B.A.* N.S. 2, 1905, 142-51. Wills of Francis Layton, 1653, and Henry Layton, 1702; rental of lands in Rawdon, Horsforth and Yeadon, c. 1702(?) and bill of complaint by Thomas Rookby and William Smith, 1723, relating to probate.

Ledes

SKAIFE, ROBERT H. 'Testamentum Willelmi de Ledes, filii et heredis Rogeri de Ledes, factum', *Y.A.J.* 17, 1902-3, 55-8. 1400; includes pedigree. Also includes will of Jane Hussey, of North Hall, Leeds, proved 1597.

Lee

'Original documents', *Reliquary* **2**, 1861-2, 161-2. Probate inventory of George Lee of Sheffield, 1649.

'[Probate inventory of Roger Lee of Sheffield, 1614]', *Reliquary* **2**, 1861-2, 231-2.

Levet

SANBORN, V.C. 'Thomas Levet and Richard Berry', *Genealogist* N.S., **31**, 1915, 79-93. 17th c., includes wills of Thomas Levett of High Melton, 1622, Richard Berry, 1651, etc.

Lingard

BERRELL, A.M. 'The Lingard will', *Manchester genealogist* **18**(1), 1982, 13. Will of James Lingard of Sheffield, 1893.

Lord

ADDY, S.O. 'Three Sheffield wills at Somerset House', *T.Hunter A.S.* **2**(3), 1922, 269-70. Wills of Sampson Lord, 1537, Humfrey Pirrans of Hall Carr, 1578, and John Scolefeld, 1626.

Mallorie

'An ancient Richmond will (Sir William Mallorie, Knt., 1411)', *Northern genealogist* **2**, 1896, 48.

Metham

WRIGHT, JOHN. 'The will of Francis Metham of Wiganthorpe', *Y.A.J.* **8**, 1884, 367-76. 1596; includes *inquisition post mortem.*

Middleton

CROSSLEY, E.W. 'Two seventeenth century inventories', *Y.A.J.* **34**, 1939, 170-203. Probate inventories of William Middleton of Stockeld, 1614, and Sir William Ingilby, 1617.

Oldroyd

NUSSEY, JOHN. 'The will of trooper Oldroyd of Heckmondwike: an incident in the Civil War', *Y.A.J.* **59**, 1987, 95-101. 1643.

Oliver

CROSS, CLAIRE. 'York clerical piety and St. Peter's School on the eve of the Reformation', *York historian* **2**, 1978, 17-20. Primarily a transcript of the will of Richard Oliver, 1535.

Palmer

'The will of Richard Palmer of Naburn', *Reliquary* N.S., **8**, 1894, 177-8. 1543.

Pawlet

'Will of Charles Pawlett first Duke of Bolton', *T.R.S.* **11**, 1943, unpaginated (5pp.) Of Langley Hall.

Pawson

NORCLIFFE, C.B. 'The Pawson inventory and pedigree', in *Miscellanea* [2]. *T.S.* **4**, 1895, 163-8. Probate inventory of John Pawson of Kirkgate, 1576, with folded pedigree, 16-18th c.

Pigott

BRAMHALL, GEOFFREY. 'Dame Margaret Pigott (died 1485)', *R.H.* **1**(9), 1992, 2-7. Will, with brief pedigree., *etc.*

Pinder

'An old Whitby inventory', *Y.N.Q.II.* **2**, 1906, 76. Probate inventory of Samuel Pinder, 1703.

Pirrans

See Lord

Preston

PRESTON, WILLIAM E. 'John Preston: a Bradford tradesman of the 17th century', *Y.N.Q.II* **5**, 1909, 123-4. Includes probate inventory, 1694.

Rayner

CODDINGTON, JOHN INSLEY. 'The Rayner family of Batley, Co. York, and of New England', *New England historical and genealogical register* **109**, 1955, 5-11. Includes 16 Rayner family wills *etc.,* 16-17th c.

Richardson

'Richardson wills', *Y.C.M.* **4**, 1894, 92-102. List, 17th c.

Richmond
'Unpublished wills (10)', *R.H.* 2(6), 1994, 123. Will of Nicholas Richmond, 1597.

Ripley
'Unpublished wills (2)', *R.H.* 2(2) 1993, 26-7. Will of Christopher Ripley, 1598.
'Unpublished wills (6)', *R.H.* 2(4), 1993, 81. Will of William Ripley of Ripon, 1684.

Robinson
CALDERCOURT, BARBARA. 'Where there's a will ...', *J.Cl.F.H.S.* 5(10), 1994, 31-2. Extracts from the will of Thomas Robinson of Hartlepool and West Glaisdale, 1912.
See also St. Quinton and Wordsworth

St. Quinton
BROWN, WILLIAM. 'Old wills from Harpham', *T.E.R.A.S.* 21, 1915, 70-79. Medieval wills of the St. Quinton family; also of Robert Robinson of Thirnholme, 1563.

Scatcher
'The will of Matthew Scatcher, 1608-1690', *Cameo* 1996, no.1, unpaginated; 1996, no.2, 9-11. Of Morley.

Scolefeld
See Lord

Sellers
SEARLE, JOYCE. 'Will extracts', *Bod-kin* 25, 1991, 18-19. Will of William Sellers of Horton, 1851.

Slater
PURVIS, J.S. 'A long-lost York will', *Y.A.J.* 42, 1971, 53-5. Will of Thomas Slater, made in 1544.

Smyth
'The will of John Smyth of Cottingham', *Reliquary* N.S., 7, 1893, 109-11. 1504; includes brass.

Staveley
'Unpublished wills, (1)', *R.H.* 1(10), 1992, 3-5. Will of William Staveley, gent., of Ripon Park, 1598.
See also Farnham

Stonehouse
HANSOM, JOSEPH S. ed. 'The will of Christopher Stonehouse of Dunsley, in the parish of Whitby, a noted recusant, *circa* 1564-1631,' in *Miscellanea* 5. C.R.S. 6. 1909, 73-4.

Sykes
'Sykes wills', *Y.C.M.* 3, 1893, 233-5. 15th c.

Tenison
TENISON, C.M. 'Tenisonia', *M.G.H.* 3rd series 2, 1898, 33-8 & 118-24. Of Yorkshire and Norfolk, *etc.,* mainly wills.

Thompson
Thompson wills: a list of Thompson wills in the Archdeaconry of Richmond, 1750-1817, York Prerogative court, 1760-1840, Canterbury Prerogative Court, 1750-1841, and abstracts of Thompson wills and administrations. [n.p.] [n.d.] Not seen.

Thoresby
FORD, J. RAWLINSON. 'Probate of Ralph Thoresby's will', in *Miscellanea* 1. *T.S.* 2. 1891, 149-50. 1725.

Thwaites
OLIVER, W. 'A local postmaster of the 17th century: Christopher Thwaites of Greta Bridge, 1626?-1693', *T.R.S.* 10, 1943, unpaginated (2pp.) Includes will, 1692.

Tymerman
'The will of Bernarde Tymerman of Hull, organ maker, 1535', *Reliquary* N.S., 8, 1894, 176-7.

Vavasour
MACDONALD, HILDA A. 'Will of William Vavasour of Stead in Burley', *B.A.* 9; N.S., 7, 1952, 100-104. 1642.

Waite
THREADGOULD, STAN, ed. 'Will of John Waite, butcher, died May 1604', *Don. Anc.* 2(4), 1984, 123-6. Of Fishlake.

Warton
HALL, ELISABETH, ed. *Michael Warton of North Bar House, Beverley: an inventory of his possessions, with some other inventories from the area of Beverley and Hull.* Hull: Centre for Regional and Local History, University of Hull, 1986.

Wharton

EVANS, JOAN. 'An inventory of Thomas Lord Wharton, 1568', *Archaeological journal* **102**, 1945, 134-50.
'Wills of the Wharton family', *Herald & genealogist* **1**, 1863, 261-4. Wills of Thomas Lord Wharton, 1568, and his widow Anne, 1585, of Healaugh, Yorkshire, and of Westmorland.

Whiteley

WHITELEY, STEPHEN. 'The Whiteleys of Rishworth: some early wills, 1535-1665', *T.Hal.A.S.* **4**, 1996, 49-57. Includes abstracts of 24 wills.

Wicliffe

'Wicliffe of Wicliffe', *Northern genealogist* **1**, 1895, 139. Will of Francis Wicliffe, prisoner of York Castle.

Wilkes

HEWETT, MARY. 'The Wilkes family', *Bodkin* **43**, 1996, 16-17. Will of Mary Wilkes, 1671.

Wilkinson

POCOCK, S. 'Slaidburn calling!', *Y.F.H.* **17**(1), 1991, 26-7. Extracts from the will of Leonard Wilkinson of Slaidburn, 1848, including lists of his tenants in Slaidburn, Newton, and Easington, *etc.*

Winksley

'Unpublished wills (a)', *R.H.* **2**(6), 1994, 122-3. Will of Francis Wood of Winksley, gent., 1683.

Wood

'Beneficiaries of Thomas Wood of Skelton (1822)', *R.H.* **2**(3), 1993, 52.

Wordsworth

'Wordsworth of Wadworth and London', *Y.N.Q.I* **1**, 1888, 161-66. Includes wills of Josias Wordsworth, 1776, Arthur Robinson of Hull, 1792, various deeds, *etc.*

Wrathall

'Some Wharfedale wills', *B.A.* **6**; N.S., **4**, 1921, 150. Wills of William Wrathall of Thorpe, 1595, and John Wrathall of Girsington, 1607.

D. *Inquisitions Post Mortem*

During the medieval period, an *inquisition post mortem* was made following the death of tenants in chief. For a general study based on them, see:

ROSENTHAL, JOEL T. 'Heirs ages and family succession in Yorkshire, 1399-1422,' *Y.A.J.* **56**, 1984, 87-94.

Abstracts of many *inquisitions* have been printed by the Yorkshire Archaeological Society:

BROWN, WILLIAM, ed. *Yorkshire inquisitions of the reigns of Henry III and Edward I. Vol. 1.* Y.A.S., R.S. **12**. 1892.
Yorkshire inquisitions vol. II. Y.A.S., R.S. **23**. 1898. For 1275, 1277 and 1283-95.
BROWN, WILLIAM, ed. *Yorkshire inquisitions vol. III.* Y.A.S., R.S. **31**. 1902. For 1245, 1282 and 1294-1303.
BROWN, WILLIAM, ed. *Yorkshire inquisitions vol. IV.* Y.A.S., R.S. **37**. 1906. For 1300-1307.
BAILDON, W.PALEY, & CLAY, J.W., eds. *Inquisitions post mortem relating to Yorkshire, of the reigns of Henry IV and Henry V.* Y.A.S., R.S. **59**. 1918.
A catalogue of the inquisitions post mortem for the county of York, for the reigns of James I and Charles I, in the Courts of Chancery and of Wards and Liveries. Y.A.S., R.S. **1**. 1885, 1-47.

See also:

HARRISON, B.J.D. 'Fourteenth century *inquisitions post mortem* for the Cleveland area. *C.T.L.H.S.B.* **44**, 1983, 22-6; **45**, 1983, 45-51; **46**, 1984, 27-9. Summarises 'extents' for Langbaurgh Wapentake.

SANTANIELLO, JOE. 'I remember it well: six medieval Holderness inquests', in CROWTHER, JAN, & CROWTHER, PETER, eds. *Collected articles from the Bulletin of the East Yorkshire Local History Society, nos. 1-55, 1970-Feb. 1977.* [ ]: the Society, 1997, vol. 2, 52-5. Originally published in the *Bulletin* **54**, 1996, 18-21. Discussion of mid-14th c. *inquisitions post mortem.*

Armytage

'Armytage of Kirklees: abstracts of *inquisitions post mortem ...*', *M.G.H.* N.S., **2**, 1877, 185-7. 16-17th c.

Furnival

CURTIS, EDMUND. 'Sheffield in the fourteenth century: two Furnival *inquisitions*', *T.Hunter A.S.* 1(1), 1914, 31-56. *Inquisitions post mortem* of Thomas de Furnival, 1332, and William de Furnival, 1383.

Redman

'Redman evidences', *Northern genealogist* **6**, 1903, 6-62. *Inquisitions post mortem* from Lancashire, Carlisle and Yorkshire.

Author Index

Family Name Index

Place Index

82

Overseas

Australia
Victoria 14

United States
Maine, Sanford 14